Maybe This Will Save Me

Maybe This Will Save Me

A Memoir of Art, Addiction and Transformation

Tommy Dorfman

HANOVER
SQUARE
PRESS

HANOVER
SQUARE
PRESS™

Recycling programs
for this product may
not exist in your area.

ISBN-13: 978-1-335-49856-4

Maybe This Will Save Me

Copyright © 2025 by Tommy Dorfman

Some names and identifying characteristics have been changed.

All rights reserved. No part of this book may be used or reproduced in any manner whatsoever
without written permission.

Without limiting the author's and publisher's exclusive rights, any unauthorized use of this
publication to train generative artificial intelligence (AI) technologies is expressly prohibited.

This publication contains opinions and ideas of the author. It is intended for informational and
educational purposes only. The reader should seek the services of a competent professional for
expert assistance or professional advice. Reference to any organization, publication or website does
not constitute or imply an endorsement by the author or the publisher. The author and the publisher
specifically disclaim any and all liability arising directly or indirectly from the use or application of
any information contained in this publication.

TM and ® are trademarks of Harlequin Enterprises ULC.

Hanover Square Press
22 Adelaide St. West, 41st Floor
Toronto, Ontario M5H 4E3, Canada
HanoverSqPress.com

Printed in U.S.A.

for mom and dad

Maybe This Will Save Me

a memory
without blot of contamination must be
an exquisite treasure

—Charlotte Brontë

I therefore invite you to join me with what is divine within you. If you become like me, you will be able to enter into me. Your suffering is impure, your past is impure; do not come to me polluted. Free yourself from that state, because impurity is an illusion, just like guilt. Accept the virginal splendor of your Being!

—"If the High Priestess spoke" from
The Way of Tarot: The Spiritual Teacher in the Cards
by Alejandro Jodorosky and Marianne Costa

PROLOGUE

summer 2020

She is thirteen feet tall, rail thin, draped in blush organdy attached to a pearl belt, just under her collarbones. She is hovering in the air, across the room from me, holding a book that I can't make out. Her expression is stoic, her approach stealthy. She is The High Priestess, and she is staring at me. She is the seen and the unseen, the darkness and the light—she is all things, and she will not let me pass. A diaphanous veil frames her face, behind which little can be discerned, and I can see in her eyes that this is how it must be. On her head rests a sharp crown. I start to speak, but I cannot. In my throat there is no voice. I try to move, but again, I cannot. My mind races; my body is stuck. I have been here before—how many times? I know I have seen her face, and yet I cannot recall it. Then she exhales, and the air she breathes is both whimsy and war, both mirth and might, both love and loss, and as I feel this cool wind rush past me, she reaches for the veil—

BEEP. BEEP. BEEP.

I wake with a start, shake my head, blink as if trying to get rid of a spiritual film clouding my eyes.

I saw her so clearly. Her.

But then she was gone.

I'm sitting in near darkness, and it takes my eyes a moment to readjust to reality. I'm in a house on Whitefish Lake, in a well-appointed guest room where I've been so graciously put up on vacation with Kaia and her family. In the light of day, the room was beautiful and welcoming, its eastward-facing windows offering a sweeping vista of the pine-laden mountains. But now, with the thick blinds still shut and only a faint sliver of light peeking in, it feels somehow strange, more ominous.

I take a second to wiggle my toes, to remind myself that I exist in the here and now—but I'm still reeling from my dream. It felt so real, seemed so present—and that scares me. As of late, my dreams have been unnaturally vivid, as if I'm not just dreaming, but caught up in a moment, experiencing something. Do I have a tumor? Are these acid flashbacks? I'd read online once that LSD never leaves your spinal cord. I've been sober for nearly ten years, but maybe my body held on to a little something, like trauma stored in a muscle, and now my hormone pills are releasing it.

Truth be told, these visions aren't even the strangest thing happening to me at the moment. I mean, what's a mild hallucination when your dick might be atrophying? Only, I'm in the process of learning how to no longer think of it as a "dick"—and that's disorienting, too, even though in my heart, I know it feels right.

Earlier that day, Kaia's boyfriend took a picture of me posing in a white floral dress. I was draped across a lounge chair situated at the edge of the water, the slightest fold of my still-masculine buttock peeking out from beneath the fabric. It wasn't exactly giving Venus, but there was something about the way the strap blithely hung off my shoulder that made me feel incredibly sexy in a completely new way. If you showed that picture to nearly anyone else in the world, they'd see a man in women's clothing. My face still has traces of a five o' clock shadow, and my hair is short and tousled.

I, however, for the first time in my life, saw a woman. Or at least a version of myself closer to womanhood, a freedom that I'd longed for since...well, forever.

At this point, I'm only two weeks into taking hormones, something that only my closest friends know. I haven't even told my parents or my husband yet. The past six years, prior to starting my medical transition, I lived in a gender-fluid, non-binary space both publicly and privately. It was a liminal space that bought me time before committing fully to womanhood. The thought of having to make this public makes me want to disappear, but ultimately, being an actor who has made even the slightest dent in the industry doesn't afford me the opportunity to transition in private forever. At some point the day will come when I'll have to clarify for the world who I am before the world decides without my consent. I envy the dolls who transitioned earlier in their lives or careers, working stealth in our industry or so inarguably passable their femininity isn't up for debate. This wouldn't be my reality and for the past three or four years, I've been contemplating a medical transition, knowing damn well there was a girl inside banging against the walls of my soul, rattling my bones, raising its eyebrows at my Grindr profile—desperate to be seen and heard and valued. Desperate to be loved by others and by myself.

I knew I was a girl from the time I was three years old. I spent years hiding that femme soul in middle and high school, up until the end of college, when I came out as non-binary. I convinced myself that this was where the buck stopped, that I was just a sexually fluid androgyne with a penchant for slip skirts and Balenciaga heeled boots. It took a trans girl moving into my house in LA and seeing my femininity clear as day for me to accept the fact that, at some point, if I was going to live at all, it would have to be as a woman. Nearly every trans girl I met in Hollywood clocked me, each pecking their beaks into the porcelain thin shell of my egg, nudging me—sometimes gently, sometimes fiercely—to crack.

I'll never forget the calm, knowing look on her face as she stared at me from across our patio table, cigarette smoke circling our heads at our bungalow in Los Feliz, and asked a me a straightforward question:

How do you see yourself at eighty?

It was something I'd never considered, but now that I'd been prompted, I sure as fuck didn't see myself as an old, wrinkly man. I sobbed and lamented all the reasons why I couldn't transition—my husband and career at the top of the list. But the admission, once spoken, stirred my bones and I spent the next few years oscillating between fight and flight mode, running away from the truth and deepening my masculine presentation, like a method actor, battling *her*.

Until the pandemic hit. The world stopped and I was trapped with nothing to distract me from the dysphoria monster that I'd worked so hard to keep trapped inside. Within a month of lockdown, I'd made an appointment to see a specialist at Cedars Sinai, a hospital in Los Angeles, mostly made famous by their track record of celebrity births.

From the outside, it probably feels a bit hasty, but (aside from the fact that this is the culmination of a lifetime of repressed emotion) I'm also primed for change. My world is being turned upside down. On top of the global traumas, I'm edging closer to a divorce.

My marriage still technically exists on a few pieces of notarized paper in the Portland, Maine, clerk's office, but my husband, Peter, and I have been separated (on and off) since last year. At this point, I know it's over, but we're still going through the motions. Nonetheless, I'm terrified of life without him. I care about him more than anything or anyone, and it makes me sick thinking of how much time we've invested into each other and our shared life. For the past year or so, though, whenever I wake up before him in the morning, I watch him sleep, the whole time thinking about how he deserves so much more love than I could ever give him in this lifetime.

In other words, I have a lot going on.

It's not like I planned it this way, and I can't really tell if one thing led to the other—or vice versa. Whatever the case, having all of this happen at once is emotional whiplash. On the one hand, I feel so much clarity, like I'm finally on my way toward becoming the person I was always meant to be. On the other hand,

I feel desperately confused, filled with heady new feelings, and thoughts, and questions—questions that nobody seems to have the answers to.

This is to say nothing of my broader, more socially oriented concerns. Even though it's the most radical act of self-love I've ever undertaken, assuming the mantle of trans-femininity means I am stepping into the eye of a raging, potentially violent storm. The unfortunate truth is that the very foundation of my existence will be condemned by a fearful, yet vocal (and powerful) minority.

Here's the thing, though: I've always been a loud-ass bitch. Ask anyone who knows me. Ask my family. Ask my friends. Ask my foes. I speak from the heart, from the gut, and when I laugh, I laugh boisterously, and it echoes across rooms and makes whoever is with me hide their face in their palms. I do not plan on going silently into this transfemme night.

Still, I need guidance.

These disparate factors and forces all seem to converge now here at Whitefish Lake. In fleeing Los Angeles—and ostensibly, my problems—I'm hoping to see it all from afar, to uncover both the strange idiosyncrasies and the startling universalities of what I'm experiencing.

And that is why, on this crisp Montana morning, I find myself rummaging around the mess in my suitcase in search of a deck of tarot cards.

Tarot has, for the past few years, been a bedrock in my spiritual practice. And while I've invested time and energy into pulling daily cards for myself, and cards for others, I am still no expert. But I find comfort and often clarity in these seventy-eight cards.

Tarot has also given me a way into my past and kept me grounded and inspired to move into a brighter, more productive, possibly less depressed and anxious future. I didn't grow up with Jesus or religion, I grew up with agnostic parents who raised us to be practical, durable Irish-Catholic-Russian-Jewish function-ing alcoholics in the twenty-first century. The functioning part missed me and I fell down a rabbit hole of drugs, sex, and Britney Spears's only perfect album, *Blackout*. From twelve to twenty-one I was a coke-monster tornado wreaking havoc everywhere, up and down the East Coast, a little to the West, and a summer in Europe with my first love. Until I reached twenty-one and decided that I didn't need to dig deeper into a bottom, the bottom found me.

With sobriety came spirituality. And looking for substance during a dark deep depression, four years sober having just moved to LA, I was obviously introduced to tarot and rose quartz butt plugs. At none other than Young Hollywood's most commanding, and terrifying, starlet's Halloween party, a tiny Venice Beach Instagram witch with four-week-old glitter pulled me into a small room and read my cards for the first time. She was clearly unhinged, but the cards did not lie. Possible divorce, gender confusion, writing, death, love, life, everything was on the table—my past, present, and future—and I was hooked. Vulnerable and open, I dove deep into the world of tarot and she offered me answers, ways into my life and the world that I couldn't get to on my own.

Though I've only been here for a night, I already feel a deep connection to Whitefish Lake. The mountain air is fresh, filled with the smell of sap and murmurous sounds of animal life. To do a tarot pull inside, when I'm surrounded by such incredible natural energy, feels disrespectful. I head out onto the veranda to which my room is attached and attempt to create a sacred space on the large iron table that looks out over the lake. I place the cards down, as well as a cheap Reiki candle I found at a gift shop in town. I figure it's the thought that counts. Also in my hands is a bundle of sage, a light woo-woo, witchy slay. I light it up and begin to slowly move around the veranda, allowing the fragrant smoke to billow about. I always feel somewhat ridiculous burning sage, but if nothing else, the smell calms me. I don't know if it's because it actually calms me, or because I've been taught to think that it calms me; who am I to question a good thing?

When the space feels appropriately cleansed, I take a seat.

Something about doing this pull feels so momentous, as if what it reveals will immediately calcify into destiny. What if I don't like what the cards have to say? The only thing stronger than my desire for answers is my fear of revelations. Yet, I know that there's no sense in running from the cards. They aren't magical talismans that are going to place a hex on me if I make one wrong step. That's not how tarot works. Tarot is about interpreting the messages that are already being sent, making sense of the vibrations that are already in the ether. Tarot is the lens through which the writing on the wall becomes clear.

Which brings us back to The High Priestess: arguably the wisest, most spiritually sound character in all of tarot. Enlightened, a keeper of divine knowledge, unnervingly wise and poised. All things I feel I don't have, aspirational qualities still light-years away. There was a brief moment in my early twenties, after I'd gotten sober and married Peter, where I thought I'd figured it out. Not like I was done growing or had nothing left to learn, but that I'd reached *that place*. You know *that place*. It's the place we think about our whole young lives, the magical point at which we assume it'll all *click*, and we'll achieve moral clarity, and life will make sense. As a kid, I remember thinking, *One day, I'll get it. One day, I won't feel so weird. One day, I'll understand myself.* (Uh, hello, gender dysphoria.) Before it could take root, though, that sense of completion began to slowly dissipate, replaced by familiar feelings of anger and sadness and isolation.

I knew that coming out as trans wouldn't fix everything. There was no switch to be flipped that could forever rid me of negative emotion. If anything, announcing to the world that I was—and always had been—a woman was an open invitation for pain and hardship to enter my life.

The worst thing, however, about having lived out a gender charade for the past twenty-eight years was that I never felt like I've ever had a fucking clue what was going on. I've hid from my emotions, turned my back on all the strange thoughts I've had, hoping that they would simply go away. But now, having begun my transition in earnest, what had once felt like a luxury—the ability to hide—now seems a terrible burden. I don't want to carry this reflex with me into womanhood. I'm determined to get to know the real Tommy, to trace the shape of my scars, to solve all the crimes I've perpetrated against myself.

And this really scares me.

Out on the water, a cool breeze begins to blow, forming swathes of delicate ripples that cause the surface to shimmer like a mirage. I reach for the deck and begin to shuffle it. Somewhere in the distance, a bird sings. As the cards slide through my hands, I pray to the spirits, whoever and wherever they are. Ahead of any pull, as you're shuffling the deck, it's crucial that you not only visualize the question you want answered, but allow yourself to truly feel the emotion at the heart of your quandary. You're supposed to repeat the question to yourself—internally or externally—over and over again. This allows it to find its footing, to organically coalesce, and as the wind rolls off the water and sweeps across my tightly scrunched eyelids, a question begins to take shape:

Who...am...I?

My lungs expand, and chills run down my neck and shoulders. Suddenly, my fingers start tingling. I know to stop at this moment, split the deck in three, and splay the cards out in a disorganized fashion. A voice comes into my head—*nine*—then leaves just as quickly. I allow that instinct to guide me, and within seconds, there are nine cards on the table before me.

Shit.

I can't make sense of them at all. There doesn't seem to be a coherent thread, no narrative woven through them that I can latch onto. I'm hit with a wave of embarrassment. What the hell was I thinking this would accomplish? Was this a total waste of time?

I look back out at the water, spot the little folds of white scattered amongst deep blue. I light a cigarette and pull at my thumbnail with my teeth. Those waves, seemingly random striations...

You're probably rolling your eyes. *Of course nothing was going to happen, you dumb bitch. It's not real!* I think of it as a looking glass, a way of accessing memories and bringing them into focus; a tool kit for clarity in the present; an offering of what could be in the future. For now, I focus on the past. After all, memories are muddy.

Sometimes, I carry myself away with the magic of tarot and forget that I, too, was once like you (probably) are: Skeptical. A nonbeliever.

But that's okay. Tarot isn't an exact science. It's meant to be something that we can each imbue with our own special sense of meaning. After all, memories are muddy.

An example: I recently asked my brother about the time he lit all my girl's clothes on fire in elementary school; he belly laughed.

T! That was you!

This left me despondent, because for years, I had been living in an alternate reality, thinking that one of my greatest childhood traumas was of my brother's making. But to find out at twenty-eight that it was my own hands that set my feminine wardrobe aflame made me question, well, *everything.* Was I just so embarrassed—or traumatized—by the experience, that I needed to pin the destruction on someone else?

A large gust causes the trees to rustle, and I once again inspect the cards. Strange. Maybe this is an archaeological endeavor, an attempt to excavate everything I've buried. Dysphoria and dysmorphia have shrouded my entire life in darkness until very, very recently, and still, my body has not been completely rid of their wrath. So much of my past remains as a mystery to me—but I'm recovering. Or, at least I'm trying to. So what do I want from this? I take a long drag from my cigarette.

These cards don't have to provide me with answers, but I need them to show me which questions I ought to be asking today and in the future, like a road map for a new beginning, I need their guidance. I need their help.

So I turn to the first one.

SIX OF CUPS

upright: revisiting the past, childhood memories,
innocence, joy

reversed: living in the past, forgiveness,
lacking playfulness

I reach for the first card—the Six of Cups.

In it, a young boy stoops low to pass a cup filled with flowers to an even younger girl. There's another cup resting on a pedestal behind them, and lining the courtyard in which they stand are yet another four.

The boy's eyes are kind, and filled with a beautiful sadness. The way the flowers billow out of the cup seems to me almost like a flame, the cup like a torch.

Behind them, an old man strides gracefully away, back into a parapeted tower that rises high into the air. It reminds me of something...

SEBASTIAN

Atlanta is a city in the forest, and on this early summer evening, the skyline looms over the treetops like medieval spires. I find myself sitting on the outside patio at Bookhouse, one of my old haunts. My cousin Tasha informed me earlier in the day that it's going to be torn down to make way for another live/work/play apartment complex. I try to flesh it out in my mind's eye as I light a Parliament: almost assuredly a five-over-one cube with, I don't know, a sleek white facade and red accents.

It feels right. Not *good*, but expected. This whole strip of Ponce de Leon Avenue—replete with iconic spots like Clermont Lounge and The Local (I'd originally intended to go there, but the crowd of bro-y bankers lurking outside gave me pause)—was up for grabs. Developers had even reclaimed "Murder Kroger" and made it just, well, a regular Kroger? Stuffed with craft beers, canned Blue Bottle Cold Brew, fresh flowers, and parking for your electric scooter off the BeltLine. I saw someone on FKA Twitter call buildings like these "blandmarks." Oy vey.

The smoke from the Parliament starts to curl, billowing back toward me and stinging my eyes. Sort of a masochistic tease.

Thing is, I have to quit smoking altogether. I need to. But one thing at a time.

First, I need to reckon with the fact that my legacy will soon be laid to rest.

By legacy, I mean the years in high school I spent drunk driving from El Bar, to Star Bar, to MJQ to whatever after-hours we could find, then breaking my fast with a mediocre waffle covered in overprocessed syrup at Majestic Diner before heading straight to school, a dehydrated mess. All this via Ponce. Memories of childhood car pools, then later, fucking in back seats, racing over construction cones, blasting Lady Gaga's *The Fame*, that my friends and I had illegally pirated and burnt onto a CD after its release. All of this to be washed away.

I wonder if it'll be like *Poltergeist*:

You built the houses, but you left the faggots, didn't you?!

These memories are seared into my mind like long exposures—streaks of lights among blurry nights—and it's clear that I can't go down memory lane alone. This is like a trauma hallway, and the door I need to get into—the really important one, with all of the good, painful shit—has been locked.

By me. And I threw away the key.

I'm back in Atlanta for the explicit purpose of trying to dredge up everything I've repressed. I'm not sure I'm ready for this. Hell, I'm not even sure I *want* to do it at all. But I'm east of thirty now. My knees are getting shotty. I can't run anymore.

If I want this trip to be anything other than a half-baked *Euphoria* prologue (*Tommy was three the first time she wore a dress...*), I need to talk to someone who has a copy of the key that will open up the door I locked so very long ago.

I need Sebastian.

He answers my phone call almost immediately.

"Oh my God," he says. "Tommy Dorfman."

His voice is like a salve for the soul. Smooth as ever, but just enough spunk to give you a little surge of energy. I tell him what's going down, and he says he'll be there in five.

When he pulls up in his black Audi SQ5 and hops out, I'm instantly transported fifteen years back in time. He hasn't aged a goddamn day. His swarthy, cherubic face is handsome as ever, and still set beneath one of his trademark felt hats. He must be in his late thirties, because he was quite a bit older than me when we met. Once he sits down and orders a glass of sauv blanc, I ask him to recount that story.

Brad told me I had to meet this new guy Tommy who was hanging around Blake's. How old would you have been? Sixteen? he asks.

I smile and nod.

Jesus Christ. But you had this gravitas about you. You were an "it" boy. Is there anything "it" in Atlanta?

Girl, everybody wanted a piece of Tommy Dorfman.

Probably because they knew I'd put out. Or pay for everything in a blackout.

That didn't hurt, but it was more than that, T. I remember walking into Felix's with you and the whole bar just going silent. There was something about you. You were always serving a wild look. And you were young and hot. It was a lot of things I guess.

I frown at him. Shame creeping up, creeping in. I don't believe him (or anybody who pays me a compliment).

I remember people being quite standoffish toward me. Like, I felt like a lot of people wouldn't talk to me. And felt like I had so much to prove.

Sebastian shrugs, *I think a lot of people were* intimidated *by you.*

This cracks me up. The thought of anyone being intimidated by me feels so strange, so anathema to the proper order of things. Like, if only you could see me at 6:03 a.m. in Brooklyn, picking up my dog's shit, then you'd realize you have nothing to worry about.

Maybe, I wonder aloud.

Definitely, he says.

Sebastian is the type of friend everybody searches for, but

so few find. You know, *a good friend.* The kind of person that builds you up, defends you, cradles you during the dark nights of your soul, and asks for nothing in return. Yet because they're so wonderful, you want to give them your all, to show them you're capable of being just as amazing of a friend, even if in reality you're a fucking mess.

We very quickly became close. After a few months of drug-fueled partying, I suddenly found him spending the night at my house, hanging around for family dinners, eventually even spending the holidays with us. I even spent a summer living in his lofted spare bedroom. It wasn't even intentional, I just never left.

I remember one day being at your house and talking to your dad and realizing, "Whoa. Tommy is, like, a real friend of mine. We're not just party buddies. I genuinely care about this person."

I felt very much the same, I say.

And then I wonder what it means that we were so close during this time in my life. I was an addict. I'd get drunk six nights a week and do drugs to get me through the seventh. I was blowing coke in the bathroom at my hippie private school; taking Molly with my voice coach on Tuesdays and Thursdays; nodding off in the Barney's Co-Op dressing room from too much champagne.

Though Sebastian partied with me and the other debaucherous gays that made up our extended circle, he never pushed things to the limit. He didn't have a taste for drugs, and would often stay sober to drive us around from bar to bar. As I study him from across the table, I recall how incredibly grounding I found him then—and I realize how grounding I find him now.

Could you tell that I was struggling? I ask.

He leans back, takes a sip of his wine, looks out at the Atlanta skyline.

Yeah… I mean, yeah. He sighs. *You were young, you know? It's hard to tell what's a genuine problem, and what's just being a wild teen-ager. But the more I got to know you, the more…yeah.*

We had a routine back then. It went something like this:

Whatever the night, we start at The Local or Bookhouse for some drinks and food. Then we roll the party over to Blake's, the infamous gay dive bar in Midtown, where I buy a couple of rounds for everybody (sometimes seemingly the whole bar), by typing my mom's credit card number, that I'd memorized, into their POS system. And lots of drugs are consumed in the bathroom. Sometimes we shut Blake's down, but if we're feel-ing antsy, we head down the street to Felix's or Oscar's, which were both busted as hell, but saucy all the same; cramped bars tucked in the back of strip malls that play gay porn instead of sports. More Jägerbombs, more coke, more mystery drugs from drag queens. If you get into Felix's before 3:00 a.m., they lock the doors, and you can keep things going until four or five. Oth-erwise, we drive the tenth of a mile that separates Felix's from my house—usually with a harem of friends and would-be lov-ers—where we keep drinking, keep doing drugs, and I usually end up getting fucked, often on the cold granite stone encasing my pool, my parents asleep upstairs with their sound machine on blast to drown out my teenage experimentations below.

Sebastian recalls one particular instance in which he was float-ing in my pool while Jack and I went at it on the ground a few feet away. I can almost feel the callous grit of the tile on my back, my body rocking back and forth with the motion of something I try to convince myself is love.

Sex was very much an escape, a mask behind which to hide myself or disappear entirely. I often felt my spirit float out of my body and watch from above; I think the term for that is disas-sociation. Whatever it is, I never stayed in my body for long. I would become a carnal shapeshifter, using the rigid contours of my bones and skin to obscure the withered shape of my soul.

Hot. Sexy. Hollow.

Already something of an exhibitionist by nature, living so fast and loose at such a young age only amplified the extent to which sex became a performance for me, a way to signal that I was mature. That I belonged. That I was worthy.

I was fourteen when I lost my virginity to a twenty-seven-year-old man I'd met on Myspace.

My older brother, Daniel, caught us the next morning as I was attempting to sneak him out our back gate. It was one of the only times he ever told my parents about something he'd seen me doing. My parents sat me down and chastised me about the dangers of what I'd done, but nothing much ultimately came of it. I begged them to not report the incident to authorities and promised I wouldn't do it again. I'm not sure they know what he and I did, only that I had an older man over.

My dad recently expressed regret that he'd never pressed charges against the man who'd made me his catamite.

This must sound irresponsible to you. Most parents would have called the police without a second thought and gone nuclear on their child. But the Dorfman household had an unorthodox approach to authority, sexuality, and most of all, supervision. Also, I begged him not to do anything rash.

Sebastian can't help but laugh at the memory of seeing me get banged cabana-style.

I was pretty amazed by the stuff we got away with at your house, he says. *Sometimes it was like, "Who's raising Tommy?"*

Sometimes it was you! I shout.

The table playing board games a few feet away all turn to look at me. I blush, but also love the fact that Sebastian and I are getting so animated. And it's at this point that I remember just how much I love him.

Sebastian was one of the few completely platonic relationships I enjoyed during my high school years. Partially because he is a decent man who understood that sleeping with an underaged teenager wasn't exactly kosher, but also because we just have this fraternal energy. We get each other. We care for each other. We look out for each other.

He is now, as he was then, a successful art director for film and TV.

Did I ever tell you I got in trouble for watching you at the Met? he says out of the blue.

I laugh, light another cigarette.

What?!

Yeah. We were deep into preproduction on a movie, working out of an office, and I had a three monitor setup. I set every single one of them to Met coverage. Like, I was not going to miss this. Then one of the producers walked by and kinda frowned.

"What's that?" he asked.

"My best friend's at the Met," I said. "But he was old and didn't really get it. Later that week, he pulled me aside and told me I couldn't be 'watching TV' at work."

I'm stunned. It strikes me as an act of such profound love. I think back to that night—the tight green rubber of my Christopher Kane dress suctioned to my nipples, the two-hundred-year-old tiara digging into my head, and uniting with my friend Kaia Gerber at the top of the steps, which became some meme about practicing witchcraft at the Met—and I refract it all through the lens of Sebastian sitting at his desk and being chastised for his joy.

I couldn't believe that you were fucking there, he says. *I was crying.*

I take a long drag of my cigarette, trying to choke back tears of my own. Maybe I wasn't such a flop after all.

How the hell did I make it out alive? How did I manage to survive those turbulent days and somehow stumble my way into the fucking Met gala? I owe a lot to privilege, that's for sure. If I wasn't born into my family of origin, I'd probably be dead. Rehab was not cheap.

But I believe it's more than that. Having the resources to get the help you need is an often necessary, but never sufficient,

condition of sobriety. No, you need a drive. A goal. Something
to live for.

As I'm working through this in my head, I feel a pang in my
boob. Classic puberty. My nipples can be tender as hell.

And then I wonder: How much do I owe my survival to the
fact that I knew there was an unrealized truth lurking within me?
That there was a woman begging to be released, just waiting to
feel the sun against her skin and the dull pain in her tits? And that
if I gave up, she would remain forever trapped?

Memories begin running through my mind in a rapid-fire
succession—drinkinginBlake's;drunkdriving;linesofblowon
aporcelainsink;adickinmyface;cryinginthecounselor'soffice;
stumblinghomeat6am;mydickinsomeone'sface;momyelling
atme;thecolorfullightsofadancefloor;thedarknessofmybedroomin
thedawn—suddenly, I stop. My hands go limp, and the cigarette
tilts toward the ground, sending a cloud of ash into my water.

But I don't care. I'm too preoccupied with a single thought:

How much of it was *her*? How much of the pain was her agonized
cry? Was she speaking through addiction?

Was she trapped in utero, gasping for air, begging to be released,
and the only way I knew how to shut her up was by drowning
her in alcohol and ketamine and poppers and opiates and God
knows what else?

The thought disturbs me, and I mourn for that little girl.

I see the coterie of bankers and real estate brokers that deterred
me from going to The Local now streaming down Ponce in a
drunken procession, their heraldry a patchwork of striped Peter
Millar polos and Sperry loafers, and I wonder if there once was
(or still is) a little girl trapped in one of them. I think of all the
ways they might have suffocated her, run from her, been paralyzed by the first rattling gasps of her breathy cries.

One of them turns and makes eye contact with me, and I can
see in his eyes that he knows what I am, that he sees my femi-

ninity, feels it in his bones with the force of a leveraged buyout. But just as quickly as the curiosity begins to spread across his face, before he can even begin to process what I make him feel—fear, envy, lust—he turns back to follow the westward arc of Ponce as it weaves its way downtown.

I light another cigarette, rest my smile upon Sebastian's kind face, and thank God and the universe for making me a woman and not a closeted financial consultant.

Then I take a drag and make a mental note to ask my agent if Sherry's wants to do a campaign with me.

WAVES

Drips of sour lemon juice slid down my neck and over my face. Above me, small, sticky hands vigorously squeezed the small yellow fruit until they're nearly unrecognizable shells. These hands belong to my cousin Carter, who, smiling, tosses the spent rinds aside.

There! That's it! By sunfall, the perfect blond will magically appear! Okay, now let's bury Helen in the sand.

We were at Holden Beach in North Carolina, the place where my family gathered each summer. For one week in June or July, the "Curran Clan"—a moniker we proudly adopted, and which I briefly intertwined with a short-lived zine I co-founded in 2023—migrated from various parts of the country to this small strip of colorful shoreline. Here, we communed, engaging in cooking competitions and basking in the sun. We bodysurfed, took long walks in ninety-five-degree weather, and playfully tormented each other. My fondest adolescent memories are from this place. I was a bit of an odd one out, sandwiched between two sets of cousins who were a few years older and younger than I was. I yearned to hang with the teenagers, sneaking drags of older relatives' cigarettes, exploring the dunes, and hunting for crabs under the moonlight. At the same time, I was comfortable playing with the younger kids, painting their faces or playing sprawling games of make-believe that would last for the duration of the trip.

Once a week, we all visited The Pavilion at Myrtle Beach, a quaint amalgamation of carnival and amusement park. This ritual in many ways defined our collective childhood. Ten of us would cram into a van, me secured on the laps of my cousins Celia and Carter. An older cousin, barely an adult, would drive. The Pavilion was magical, alive with vibrant colors, cotton candy, gravity-defying rides like the Alien Saucer and Pirate Boats, free falls, wooden roller coasters, and stuffed bears—few of which ever made it back home with me to Atlanta.

Carter and I were peas in a pod. Towheaded blondes at birth, by the time I was entering sixth grade, at which point Carter was entering high school, our hair had lost some of its luster. Her locks remained an icy blond, while mine had dulled to a strange shade of honey-meets-dirt. We discovered, however, that lemon juice would naturally lighten our hair under the sun. This was a preferable outcome to what we'd achieved the previous summer, a drab orange that resulted from an overuse of Sun In purchased at the Beach Mart.

My family visited this stretch of beach every summer since my mother was a child. Initially, it was just one house, but by the time I turned twelve, we had expanded to seven. At our peak, we numbered over a hundred, a sprawling gaggle of relatives connected by blood or marriage, all united by one goal for the week: to have fun. Any potential disruptions were swiftly quashed or pushed to the side. There was, of course, drama, but it simmered below the surface, never erupting publicly. We cooked and cleaned in teams, surfed in pairs, and spent late nights playing cornhole under the carport. Upon arriving at the beach, tradition dictated that before unloading the car, you visited each house to embrace whoever was around.

I cherished my time at the beach, not for the festivities, but for the profound sense of safety and belonging I found in my family's presence. When the world seemed harsh and friendships ephemeral, my family was my steadfast support. They were unconcerned with superficial details, more focused on connection through showering with kisses, hugs, and piggyback rides, fostering within me a fondness for nurturing that now fuels my desire to be a mother someday... Our chaotic, loud family gatherings acted as a comforting buffer against the world's darkness.

The beach was an ideal playground for a child with undiagnosed ADHD. With endless rooms to explore, people to engage with, and countless spots to retreat into my imagination, boredom was hardly ever a possibility. As I matured, however, and began to embrace my identity more confidently, the challenge of maintaining a low profile in the conservative South became harder. Concealing my pink nails in the pockets of my tiny bathing suits gradually eroded my dignity, leading me to eventually avoid these family trips altogether.

I believe this is where I first learned the significant difference between being cared for and being understood. While my family might not have grasped the complexities of gender and sexuality, their lack of understanding ironically strengthened my self-confidence as a child. Whenever discomfort arose, there were always other relatives I could turn to. The beauty of a large family lies in its ability to recognize each individual while also offering them the chance to fade into the background when needed.

But things are not the same as they once were. I am different than I was. Or at least, I am different *to them*. As a trans woman in my thirties, the prospect of joining my family in North Carolina is daunting. I'd have to discreetly adjust my appearance, use a subtle voice to prevent being misgendered—all while dodging insensitive remarks from less understanding relatives. It's emotionally taxing and potentially harmful. Yet, I remain unsure whether or not it's all in my head. Is it actually so bad? At the end of the day, my family is fiercely protective. Would they not help me through these challenges?

When I first came out at the age of fourteen, the support was overwhelming. Even the more conservative, Republican-leaning family members welcomed my truth with open arms, listened earnestly to my perspective, and showed a genuine interest in my well-being that went beyond mere curiosity. Among hundreds of relatives, I was one of only three openly queer family members. Statistically, this seems improbable, but I am not one to expose others' secrets. Or am I?

Once, when doomscrolling on PornHub, I stopped at a video of a bearded bear in training shorts. He was jacking off while chugging Bud Light (the irony not lost on me here), and he resembled my cousin so much I nearly broke my laptop slamming it shut. Once I mustered enough courage to look again, I noticed this man had a tattooed dragon on his calf and was standing in front of a Golden Gophers' jersey. This was not my cousin. I exhaled sweet relief.

Yet, as disturbed as I was by seeing a doppelganger of my cousin on a gay porn website, it strangely drove home that saddening reality that there aren't more openly queer people on my mom's side of the family. There's just my cousin Tasha who has been out as a lesbian since high school, then another cousin who came out later as bisexual, and me: the lonely trans member of the Curran Clan. I didn't have a road map to guide me through the grueling years of puberty as a gay kid and keep me on a safe path. Perhaps it would have alleviated some of the trauma, or at least softened the judgment. On the flip side, my ignorance did come in handy every now and then. Getting to use the excuse, *I didn't know I wasn't supposed to do that! Nobody told me!* And I made a lot of messy choices.

Like, in 2006, my first "out" Christmas. My parents, siblings, and I were up in Keene, New Hampshire, with the majority of my mom's side enjoying the typical icy snowscape and blacking out nightly playing beer pong, which was both accepted and celebrated in my family. My drinking progressed to nightly puking. Though I was mostly able to keep it to myself, I have some recollection of stern conversations with family about learning how to handle my liquor. Whatever, I was fourteen and doing my best.

A few days before Christmas, Carter and I, along with our other cousin Leigh Ann, ventured to the local Borders to pick up some last-minute gifts for our parents. As I fingered through the magazine section, I locked eyes with a bleached blonde babe. At this point, I'd already scored a few times cruising in Atlanta, so I felt confident in my ability to lock him in if I chose to. The challenge lay less in closing the deal than in sussing out if he actually *was* gay or just *looked* gay. In the case of the latter, I was afraid he would end up punching me if I hit on him.

He was wearing tight jeans, so that was promising, as well as a cowrie shell necklace. Also gay. His Timberlands threw me off, though. I decided to keep my eyes down and take out my new flip phone. It was a Nextel, the ones that had a walkie-talkie system that the whole family could use. I got kicked out of class multiple times because my dad couldn't resist doing a Mickey Mouse impression in the middle of his workday to send me his love. (He also had undiagnosed ADHD.)

Anyway, after about five minutes of staring at my phone, the blond boy leaned his elbow on the shelf and softly asked if he could help me, introducing himself as Chris.

Oh, I'm just killing time waiting for my family to get whatever they're... My voice trailed off.

He stared at me intently, softly smiled.

Cool. Do you live around here?

My heart began to race. Unsure what else to do, I blurted out random facts about my life, feeling it necessary to say that I was from Atlanta, but that we spent winters in New Hampshire to tap into the Christmas spirit, and that I had to go back and forth because I'm still starring in the *Nutcracker* at the ballet.

He laughed at my enthusiasm. He was a sophomore at Keene State University, he said, but preferred to stay here over the holidays than go back to the even smaller, shittier town in New Hampshire where he was from, citing differences in opinion between him and his biological family.

Especially with me being, ya know…gay and all…

My heart leaped into my throat.

Well, if you want to come hang with me and my family they're all pretty cool with it.

Really?

Yeah.

At this point, I was sweaty and struggling to conceal my boner, so I swiftly gave him my number and left the store. Once home, I sat and stared at my phone, willing it to vibrate. Hours went by without anything happening. I was embarrassed by my forwardness, so I started to drink in hopes of forgetting about what an idiot I'd been. I mean, who invites a stranger over to their home to meet their whole family? What was I thinking? I'd decided to give up on him ever reaching out.

And that was precisely when my phone finally buzzed.

Chris: Hey qt sorry took me a min to text you got the xmas rush.

With absolutely zero inhibitions (or game), I responded immediately.

Tommy: nbd what up.

Chris: Nm, ab to drive to campus. Hbu?

Tommy: Oh dinner with the fam, boring, getting drunk hehe

Chris: Jealous. Bet ur cute when ur drunk.

Tommy: I try ;-)

Chris: When can i see you?

Tommy: Tomorrow? We're having a party. You should come.

Chris: You sure that's cool?

Tommy: Totally.

Chris: How old are you?

Tommy: Guess.

Chris: 17?

Tommy: Yupppp

I mean what's a few years?

Chris: Cool. well, i think i could make it i'm done with work at like 10 though is that too late?

Tommy: Naw, perfect.

Chris: Cool.

I decided at that point this wasn't worth mentioning to my family, at least not until the next day when everybody was sober. Plus, that gave me enough time to figure out what lie I was going to tell.

So, my friend's cousin Chris is here with no family or anything. Is it cool if he comes over tomorrow?

That would do! My parents never could keep my friends' names straight anyway, and they were always incredibly inviting.

When Chris arrived, I was already significantly tipsy. The giddiness of having him over was nearly as intoxicating as my third glass of champs, a refreshing break from the usual family holiday routine. His scent—a mix of Clinique Happy and Axe deodorant—and the flannel layers he wore, fit perfectly into the festive atmosphere. His presence seemed to invigorate the evening, adding a layer of excitement.

Finally, I said pulling him into the guest bathroom in the basement. My cousins were just on the other side of the door, playing beer pong on one side of the room and *Super Mario Kart* on the other. We immediately tore into each other, ripping off shirts and belts and jeans with little care for the fabrics in an offbeat staccato pace. I dropped to my knees to suck him off as he perched on the sink. He pulled me back up after a few moments, turned me around to go down on me. Trying to anchor my drunk teenage body, I clung to a large towel bar in front of me—and within a few seconds, writhing and moaning as I was, ripped it off the drywall. Chris and I fell to the floor in a fit of collective laughter, but that didn't stop us from working toward the mutual goal of pleasure. I mounted him, spit on my hand for self-lubricant (because who needs lube when you have liquid courage) and slid his dick inside me. He grabbed my hips in his nimble hands, positioned my ass so it floated just high enough above his cock to passionately (without any finesse or rhythm whatsoever) pound into me.

Was it enjoyable? Absolutely not. Did I have the confidence to challenge his chosen method of fucking? Also no. The physical pleasure came second to the euphoric hits I got from knowing I was doing something I shouldn't be doing, and that only in-

tensified when we heard loud banging on the bathroom door.
Our fuckfest momentarily silenced. Then I started laughing hysterically, and Chris threw his hand into my mouth harder than
he probably should have. I felt my lips clash with my teeth and
the faint taste of iron blood on my tongue.

What the fuck!

Sorry—sorry—just

The pounding grew in intensity.

ONE MINUTE! I screamed in the air.

What the fuck are you doing in there, Tommy? Ah, the familiar
voice of my brother Daniel. He was goofy most of the time,
but could easily turn into a stern, protective jock if the moment
called for it. I could tell immediately based on the tenor of his
voice that this was one of those moments.

Before Chris and I could get dressed, Daniel knocked the
door open, nearly breaking the handle, and swiftly lifted Chris
up by his button-down.

Who the fuck are you? Daniel screamed into his face.

Stop, Daniel! I hopelessly pleaded.

How old are you?

Nineteen. I—

And fucking around with a fourteen-year-old?

Shit. Chris looked at me, all at once confused, afraid, and
furious.

I told him I was seventeen, it's not his fault. I tried to shift the
blame, but Daniel wasn't having it.

*That's still illegal, so get the fuck out of here, you pervert. Before I
call the police or beat your ass.*

Daniel threw Chris back down on the ground, his body flail-
ing like a rag doll. Coursing with adrenaline, he quickly re-
bounded, barely having time to gather his stuff before bolting
up the stairs. We all followed him, watched him zip through
the hallway toward the front door, then out into the dark, cold
New Hampshire night.

You're such an idiot, my brother said, his voice more distant than before. Coursing with shame, I just stared out the door, watching Chris run down the dimly lit street until his body disappeared into his shitty Honda coup. I could feel the heat of my family's eyes on me, dozens of pupils trying to piece together what the fuck had just happened. My Uncle John's voice echoed in the living room, entertaining friends and family with a joke, completely oblivious to whatever drama had ensued in the other room. I didn't want to turn around and face my cousins, so instead I walked outside and shut the door behind me. I fished in my jeans for the remains of a cigarette I knew was in there, then sought refuge in the garage, where my cousin Carter was already standing, dressed skimpily, drawing from a Marlboro Gold.

Who was that?

This guy I met at Borders yesterday.

She started laughing hysterically, breaking the tension in the air, and I softened into her embrace. Carter's ability to comfort and soothe awkwardness was unmatched. I grabbed the tumbler in her hand and chugged it. Vodka Red Bull. Yum. Then I launched into a full play-by-play of what had gone down.

The next morning, I awoke to find my dad standing in the doorway of the bedroom where I was sleeping with several other cousins. He wore a stern look.

I don't want to know what happened last night. But you broke the towel rod in the bathroom. You have the day to fix it.

Okay, sorry. I responded, half-asleep.

That's sort of how it always was when we fucked up. My parents knew we were beating ourselves up enough already, and instead of mindlessly punishing us, they sought ways to remind us that we were responsible for our actions. Break something, fix it. Get a ticket, pay it. Lie about something, fess up and move on.

Yet, I often wished for more in these moments. I longed for parental guidance, whatever that might be. Maybe a long, drawn-out conversation about right and wrong, or some moral offering or lesson beyond going to Home Depot and begging an older cousin to help me finesse a new towel bar onto the wall. In other words, I wanted consequences. *Real* consequences. I don't know why. In hindsight, my teenage years were an escalating series of attempts to get my parents to actually punish me, but I wasn't very successful. Anything that had to do with sex or dating was never dealt with all that much. My dad and I had had a stern conversation about the man I'd lost my virginity to, but nothing really came of it. They didn't know how to foster conversations about safe sex with their gay son. Nobody did. I was left to piece it together however I could, be it from porn or random boys I met at bookstores.

Not until adulthood and my first year sober did I realize the trauma I went through with these experiences, how my sweet naivety at the time was often preyed upon.

THE EMPEROR

upright: authority, establishment, structure, a father figure

reversed: domination, excessive control, lack of discipline, inflexibility

&

THE EMPRESS

upright: femininity, beauty, nature, nurturing, abundance

reversed: insecurity, overbearing, negligence, smothering, lack of growth, lack of progress

At Whitefish Lake, the sun has begun to ascend, casting long shadows across the water. I've been out here for over an hour now. Reexamining. Recontextualizing. Reliving. I trace the next card with my index finger.

The Emperor stares back at me, bearded, sitting confidently in his throne.

My phone vibrates, pulling me out of the moment. I curse myself for forgetting to turn it off, but it tracks. I'm a little whore for my phone (maybe my least favorite thing about myself). In the spirit of the pull, however, I try not to beat myself up about allowing it to intrude.

It's a text from my dad. Coincidence? I think not. The universe has

a great sense of humor. I open it to find a meme of a gay, shirtless, muscled fisherman holding a rifle.

This is what I imagine your day is like in Montana

I laugh. **Cute.** *God, I need a cigarette. I haven't told them I'm transitioning yet because I still don't know if I can do it and if I can, it's going to be for me first. I know it's not novel to say that my relationship with my parents is complicated, but it is. I love them to fucking death, of that I'm sure, but I'm also equally as sure that throughout my childhood, there were many times that they zigged when they should've zagged.*

Not that I made it easy on them. Being from the South, things could have been so much worse. I was a little faggot from the time I could talk, but I still don't think anyone in my family was fully prepared for me to come out as trans. Nevertheless, when I did, my parents made it clear that even if I was no longer their son, I would still be their light. But the truth remains that I was, for many years, the youngest boy of five children.

I hibernated in my mother's womb for weeks after her expected due date, being the Taurus that I am, and the entire process was anything but traditional. At five months pregnant, my mother's doctor spotted a cyst on her ovary. They were able to determine it was cancerous and she was left with two options: She could do nothing—causing the cancer to likely worsen—then give birth with a very, very low chance of living to see me walk; or she could remove that ovary, risk my life in utero, and have a high chance of her own survival.

While the choice wasn't easy, she did what I would've done: saved herself first so as not to orphan both her existing stepchildren and me, if I pulled through. It was a risky decision, but her gut led her to make it, and so she underwent a complex surgical procedure wherein the doctor sliced her open, pushed me to the side, removed her ovary, and stitched her back up. No wonder I overstayed my welcome. That shit was traumatic.

So traumatic that, when my mom read some article that linked natal stress to being gay, she felt like there was suddenly an answer. I'm sure she's not totally wrong, that there are stats somewhere, or at least convincing memes, that tie queerness to stress in the womb—as well as being a younger sibling—so if we're basing it off that then it's not an entirely invalid way to make sense of your child being different. I'd take any excuse I could to explain away my alcoholism, trannyism, homosexualism, all the isms. As I enter my thirties, though, my need to both take responsibility for and move on from trauma feels more pertinent than ever.

I look down at The Emperor card again. A voice in my head whispers, There's no emperor without The Empress.

Goddammit. It's almost too on the nose, too perfect. I look at my phone, the text from my dad, a rueful smile on my face. At the same time, I'm struck by a peculiar thought: I'm now older than Uncle Tommy was when he passed away. For the first time in my life, I'm truly able to understand the magnitude of his death, and I see why it destroyed my parents.

Who were my mom and dad then? Who were they before I came around? When they were young, and restless, and looking to buck like wild horses?

This I need to know.

Because who are we without the trauma we inherit from the people who taught us how to live?

But I need distance. I need to see their story from the outside. I need to see it unfold like a story that I can't put down.

So let me try.

A FABLE

On the evening of May 12th, 1992, dark clouds descended upon
the city of Atlanta. It'd been a hot, muggy day, the kind that
hinted at the coming of summer, and by sunset, the heat had
spawned distant thunderheads that rumbled with discontent.

Downtown, a 37-year-old man stared out the window of a
small, quiet hospital room, surveying the twilight. Would it
rain? Would it storm? Even more pressingly, was it an omen?
Behind him, his wife lay on a narrow hospital bed, enceinte and
on edge. Next to her, with his hand delicately draped over her
swollen womb, sat her dying brother.

The man turned to look at them both, inhaling sharply so as
not to let any cracks show, at least not more than they already
had. He needed to be strong, to maintain his poise, to show everyone that it was all going to be just fine. But then his brother-
in-law smiled at him, shook his head, raised his eyebrows.

Isn't this some shit?

The man couldn't help but smile back. He recalled the first
time they'd met, at a dive bar in rural New Hampshire, the
man's wife passed out in the car because she'd been so afraid to

introduce him to her family that she overshot dinner by one or three glasses of wine. Her brother seemed just as full of life now as he did then, but it occurred to the man they might never share another drink. And then he could feel a lump forming in his throat, like a stuck lozenge plugging any possible exit for the million odd emotions churning around in his gut.

He looked at his wife now, drowsy under the influence of all kinds of drugs. With her billowing, straw-red hair, and head tilted just so against the pillow, he thought she looked an awful lot like a Renaissance painting of the Madonna, which was a rather strange thing for a Jew to notice—even one who'd celebrated Christmas his whole life.

For a moment, he felt a strong desire to climb in the bed, all six-foot, 205 pounds of him, and hold her in his arms. But he was powerless. He could only hope for the best, both for her and her brother. Suddenly, he felt very small.

His wife's eyes faintly opened, and she let out a weary chuckle. Something in her smile reminded him of the first time he'd ever laid eyes on her. How she held her mouth so delicately, so joyously.

That felt so long ago now. How had they come to this point? To this stormy Southern night? To the eve of a birth which death would soon make an even account of?

He rested his eyes and tried to think.

★ ★ ★

Catherine Mary Elizabeth Curran was born on October 14th, 1963, in Florida.

In between Cathy's cries, her mother, Celia, could be heard breathing a sigh of relief. Across the hospital room, Celia's husband, Ranger Curran Sr. did the same. The last two decades of his and Celia's life had now seen the birth of ten children, and they'd decided that ten ought to be about enough.

The Currans were a family always on the move. Air Force brats the lot of them, they'd never be in one place for too long.

All but two of them were born in different states. In many ways, this was the price of success. Ranger was a decorated Air Force pilot, who saw combat in three wars and flew as an inaugural member of the country's first jet aerobatics team, The Minute Men. To hear the children tell it, though, it wasn't much of a price at all. Sure, it made certain things like making friends tricky, but it also fostered a sense of closeness and cohesion that none of them would have traded for "stability." They truly were a clan, a world apart, speaking a language only they could speak, following a path only they could see. The family culture was as brutally honest as it was filled to the brim with unconditional love, and at any given moment, both were likely to be equally on display. To an outsider, it might have seemed idiosyncratic, but Celia always chalked it up to the fact that they were Catholic.

When Cathy was three, Ranger decided it was time to stop living with his head in the clouds, and retired from the Air Force. Not wanting to slow down, he relocated the family to Athens, Georgia, to pursue a PhD in business management at the University of Georgia. Cathy's oldest siblings were by then college-aged, and several of them enrolled in classes alongside their father.

Meanwhile, she spent most of her time being looked after by her younger siblings and the broader Catholic community in Athens, which at that time was still perceived as existing on the margins. Some of Cathy's earliest memories are of summer masses in their stuffy church; of blooming baby's breath and fragrant wisterias; of long evening shadows in the sweeping expanse of their Georgia yard. It was a fine place to be a child.

The Currans were not what you might consider passive members of society. In fact, quite the opposite. Celia was an ardent supporter of the civil right's movement, and she helped organize several protests and marches during their time in Athens. This certainly did not earn the family love and affection from the town, especially not from the good ol' boys club that ran both the university and the local government.

Maybe this is why, in spite of the family's love for Athens, Ranger didn't think twice about leaving to take a job teaching at Youngstown State in Ohio. It was there that Cathy came of age. Youngstown was a bustling, steel-producing, blue-collar town surrounded by cornfields. The family spent eleven years in Ohio, their numbers slowly but surely dwindling each spring as another child graduated. This is not to say that a feeling of loss or emptiness ever took root; each holiday season, the whole family would gather in Youngstown and easily slip back into the comfortable cadence of Curran life. Cathy never stopped feeling like she was a part of something much, much bigger than herself.

She enjoyed a beautiful childhood. There was much joy and love and healthy rambunctiousness. The thing about having a nice childhood, however, is that one is rarely ready for it to end, and though Cathy was eager to see the world, she found herself plagued by a sense of uncertainty as far as questions like Where should I go? and What should I do with my life? were concerned. To complicate matters even more, she was the tenth and final child, the baby of the family. Though her parents urged her to follow her heart, she couldn't help but feel pressure not to make the wrong choice.

After much debate, she decided to attend Ohio University in Athens, Ohio, just a few hours away from home. It was far enough to feel fresh and exciting, but close enough that she wouldn't dishonor the long-standing tradition of Curran children returning to visit as often as possible.

Shortly before Cathy graduated, however, it became abundantly clear to Ranger that it was time to semi-retire. He and Celia loved Youngstown, but they were ready for something quieter. As a child, Ranger had spent his summers in a quaint cabin in the small town of Dublin, New Hampshire. The home had remained in the family, and when Cathy's oldest brother

Ranger Jr. had graduated from UGA many years prior, he and his wife Karen moved to the nearby town of Keene and set to work fixing the place up. Celia and Ranger felt it was about time to finally move in. And Celia was eager for Cathy to join them there.

A few weeks before she was set to walk across the stage and receive her high school diploma, Ranger and Celia sat Cathy down and explained the situation.

Look, dear. We're happy to have you go to Ohio University. If that's where you feel like you belong, then you should go there, and there's nothing that would make us happier. But with us being in New Hampshire, it's going to be hard for you to get home.

This scared the living shit out of Cathy. She'd spent 18 years surrounded by Currans, rarely ever more than a stone's throw away from the nearest person who loved her. The thought of going months on end living so far away from her family was utterly terrifying.

For all intents and purposes, her decision was made the moment those words came out of her father's mouth. Come August, she packed up and followed her parents to New Hampshire.

The next two years were spent in relative peace. Ranger and Celia enjoyed the slow pace of life in Keene, with Ranger often wondering aloud if they shouldn't have been here all along. For Cathy, however, things were more of a mixed bag. In January, she moved to Durham to attend UNH, hardly an hour and a half away. She quickly made friends, enjoying the freedom and freshness of college. Yet, there was something missing.

For a year or more, this absence tickled Cathy, making itself known only as shadows of doubt, brief moments of discontent. It did not have a shape. She began trying on different courses of study for size—maybe business, maybe chemistry—but none of them would stick. By the time she started studying geriatric caretaking halfway through her sophomore year, she was at her wit's end. She felt she had no purpose, and in truth, she was afraid she might never find one. It was time for a change.

That summer, she found herself in the outskirts of Atlanta, living with her sister Caroline. Meandering through Atlanta's winding hills, she would often think about life, and just what the hell she was going to do with hers. Passing by houses, each a little world of its own, she found herself fascinated by the thought of all the lives that had been lived in these places— all the lives that were yet to be lived there—and how they had existed all this time without her knowledge. Then to multiply that across the entire world, all the lifetimes are full of adventure and pain and joy.

What a thing to think of. It tickled her brain. The community of humans was so incomprehensibly large, the sheer diversity of experiences out there waiting for just one person, let alone a million, a billion, five billion. How could anyone ever hope to be in the right place at the right time? Was there even such a thing as a "right time"? She didn't know, and she suspected she never would. For now, though, she was content to wander the foothills of the Piedmont and marvel at just how funny life could be.

Cathy needed a job and her sister's best friend knew someone who was hiring lifeguards. Her name was Mindy, and she was about to forever alter the course of Cathy's life.

★ ★ ★

Cathy could hear the roar of distant thunder. She did not like it. The hospital bed was lumpy, and she couldn't get comfortable no matter how hard she tried. The air-conditioning was too cold, but beneath the covers, she was sweating something awful, causing the starched sheets to stick to her skin like paper on a dewy glass.

She let out a groan, and her brother laughed.

You doing alright there, Cath?

She shook her head, unamused. I think I'm dilating.

Do you want me to call the nurse?

That was her husband. He sounded frantic, like a coiled spring waiting to release.

No.

All she could do was sigh.

This poor child of hers. All that it's already been through without even having left her. What would the world have in store for it? Who would her baby become? She thought of her own life, her childhood, how quickly it had passed, and now she was here. What had she learned? What could she offer her baby?

Another flash of thunder. Cathy tugged at the skin beneath her chin, closed her eyes. As she did, she felt the cool touch of a hand on her forehead. A familiar hand. A calloused hand. His hand.

★ ★ ★

Eight years before Cathy clawed her way out of the womb and into the world, a young boy did the same in Brooklyn. His name was Larry Ivan, and he was born the second of five children to Arnold and Joan Dorfman. Arnold was a kosher butcher with an entrepreneurial streak, always endeavoring to improve the family's lot in life. (Joan hated the smell of meat.)

When Larry was a year old, an opportunity to secure the financial future of the family presented itself to his dad. A friend of Arnold's worked with a large office equipment company that was looking to expand into the southeast. They needed someone to head up a southern franchise, and the friend immediately thought of Arnold, renowned for his hard-nosed approach to life and business. To take on this challenge he'd have to uproot the family from New York, where the Dorfmans had resided since emmigrating from what is now Ukraine a few generations prior—and start anew in Atlanta.

Arnold didn't think twice about accepting it.

In the summer of 1956, the Dorfmans packed up everything

they could take, sold everything they couldn't, and drove down the East Coast, eventually landing in the Heart of the South.

On the whole, Larry enjoyed himself in Atlanta. He was by all accounts an inquisitive, headstrong kid. Yet, there was a duality to life in the Dorfman household, a constant roll of the dice happening in some hidden corner that Larry was not privy to. His father, though loving and ultimately fair, had a hair-trigger temper. He believed in the value of physical discipline, and would never hesitate to speak with his belts or fists if he considered Larry or his brothers to have stepped out of line.

Arnold came by his anger honestly, or at least as honestly as one can come by such a thing. His mother was among the nastiest women to have ever (dis)graced Brooklyn, full of spite and cynicism, and as Larry would later learn when he became a father himself, the legacy of one's parents casts a long shadow.

The children would often hear Arnold and Joan arguing in the kitchen. The fire in their relationship, however, came from their deep and genuine love, and from an early age Larry was shown that, above all else, and regardless of the challenges of marriage, a spouse should be your best friend.

Adding to the list of emotional contradictions, Arnold was a tremendous teacher. His work ethic was the stuff of legend, and he instilled in his children an appreciation for the value of both labor and education. When Larry would bring home a 93 on a test, his father would calmly inquire about where the other seven points had gone.

Incensed, Larry would always have a quick retort.

Aren't you satisfied? That's an A!

It's not about me, Larry. The question is, why are you satisfied not knowing about those other seven points?

Larry didn't have a good answer for this, and over the years, he would often reflect on this lesson. He eventually realized what his father was getting after, and he resolved that if he were to ever become a teacher, everyone would get an A. His logic was sound: The objective of an education is not to measure just how much information a student had retained, it was to ensure they had retained it. Thus, he would have his students take the tests over and over again until they received an A. This made far more sense to him than the arbitrary metrics and standards used to assess students in school.

By the time Larry was ten, Arnold and Joan had given him and his sister, Mindy, three more siblings—Scott, Hy, Jan. Larry quickly took to being an older brother, helping his siblings learn how to navigate the minefield of their father's emotions—as well as how to digest the veiled nuggets of wisdom that were often offered in the midst of a rapid mood swing.

The Dorfmans were relatively laissez-faire as far as rules were concerned. Arnold and Joan never fussed over their children's whereabouts. If you weren't planning on being home that night, you were just supposed to call the house early. Then, their only obligation was to be back the next day. Larry only ever broke that rule once, and after a fierce scolding that involved several blows from his father. He never broke it again.

At the age of 7, Larry began to join Arnold at his office on the weekends, where he was taught how to work on the complex check-writing machines that his dad's company sold. For his troubles, Larry would receive an allowance. Much to both Larry and Arnold's surprise, Larry found the mechanical work deeply satisfying. There was something about identifying a problem and using your own hands to fix it that felt damn good. To hear the cogs turning again, or the drive belt whirring after it'd been sputtering for hours—well, that was simply heaven.

Over the next few years, he became an expert on the check-writers. Before long, he was one of his father's top salesmen. For every machine he sold, he received $200, and in a few days of work, he could off-load ten printers, sometimes even more.

Once Larry got a taste for money—or more accurately, the

freedom that came with it—he resolved never to be without it again.

Perhaps because he had disposable income, or perhaps because he was just generally likable, Larry was quite popular in high school. It didn't hurt that he was a solid 170 pounds of muscle at 16, and even though he was young for his grade, that number only continued to grow as he neared graduation.

After graduating at the age of 17, Larry moved to Athens to attend UGA. Unsure exactly how to navigate this whole college business, he fell back on old ways, trying out for—and making—both the basketball team and football team, though he never saw playing time in basketball, he hit the field in every football game. Throughout college, Larry continued to sell his dad's machines whenever the coffers began to run dry. At the same time, AEPi—one of two Jewish fraternities on campus—also happened to have a traditional Wednesday night poker game that was at risk of shutting down on account of everyone having gone broke. (The whole fraternity was losing and winning the same $100.) When Larry came into the picture, though, everything changed. With his backing, the game turned into a campus wide phenomenon, with people from all social groups and walks of life (included, it's rumored, several professors) clamoring to secure a coveted seat at Larry's green felt table.

Larry was earning a pretty good living doing the same exact thing he'd been doing for the better part of a decade. So he decided that he wouldn't be going back to Athens in the fall.

He wound up marrying his high school sweetheart, Randi, and they had two children, Adam and Stephanie. Larry loved his kids dearly, but the marriage never seemed to settle where it ought to, and by their late 20s, he and Randi were separated.

When Adam and Stephanie were old enough, they attended The Learning Tree, a summer camp/daycare program that his sister Mindy owned and operated. Every few days, he'd take the responsibility of driving them to Doraville, where he'd watch them splash about in the water for a half hour before heading to work. Larry enjoyed this moment of respite, a time for him to sit still and listen to the sounds of his children's joy, to fully appreciate the fact that they were growing up and turning into real people with personalities and ideas and dislikes. He also enjoyed the redhead lifeguard that kept stealing his attention away.

It was about the only thing in his life that felt stable. He and Randi were separated, living out a balletic scheme in which she'd be home for two weeks with the kids while he was at an apartment up in Roswell, and then they'd quietly switch, barely missing each other as she left for her pied-à-terre and he took up residence for his two weeks at home—and on it went. They'd agreed to stay out of each other's private lives, even as they were seeing a marriage counselor once a month to determine whether or not there was anything left to salvage. In spite of their differences, they committed to keep things civil in front of the kids, who hadn't yet wised up to what was going on, which led to the first joint custody case in all of Georgia.

One summer day, Larry dropped the kids off for swim lessons and sat down on a bench by the pool.

He inhaled, closed his eyes, and when he opened them, he saw an angel.

She was across the pool, walking toward the lifeguard stand, red hair cascading past her shoulders and coming to rest on a bathing suit of almost the same shade. She had a svelte figure and a delicate face, the most delicate Larry had ever seen. In an instant, his stomach dropped. His face flushed. His mind went blank.

Who the hell is that?

It was as if he'd been struck by lightning.

★ ★ ★

Cathy had only been working for Mindy a couple of weeks when she noticed the stout, handsome man staring at her. Truth be told, she didn't really think anything of it. She got up on the stand, and when she looked back over, the man was gone.

The next day, she saw the man again, this time outside of the school. He was talking to Mindy, a kind of mischief in his eyes. As she approached, she could feel his eyes on her.

Hey, Cathy, said Mindy. This is my brother, Larry.

Larry offered a strong hand.

Larry Dorfman. How ya doing?

Cathy. Nice to meet you.

Where ya from, Cathy?

Oh, all over, I guess. But mainly Youngstown, in Ohio...

It started this casually. Pretty soon, a brief but pleasant conversation with Larry came to be a fixture of her day. He was kind, curious, always asking questions that were one or two steps deeper than before. Cathy found herself looking forward to these little exchanges. Larry was handsome, but he was eight years older than her. Plus, he was married with kids! She was just twenty years old, still unsure if Atlanta would be a permanent home or simply a way station.

The city, she had to admit, was pulling her in. She'd joined a tennis league, had established a "regular grocery store," was starting to dread driving on certain roads; things you do when you actually live in a place. Hell, sometimes she wondered if she was developing a bit of a Southern twang. God forbid...

Against this backdrop, the summer continued on, thick with heat and fragrant with the scent of magnolias. While Cathy was teaching a kindergarten class, she began applying to other jobs. The Center for Disease Control was looking for a secretary. It was a good job, something that had the potential to turn into a career, with lots of upward mobility and stable benefits. Her family encouraged her to accept it.

Mindy was sad to see her go, but understood the logic behind the move. She thanked Cathy for having been so great during her time at the school, and they settled on an agreeable last day.

★ ★ ★

She's leaving the daycare? But she's staying in Atlanta?

Mindy narrowed her eyes, and suddenly it all clicked. Her brother was smitten. She'd seen the two of them talking after lessons, had seen the way Cathy looked at Larry. She felt silly for not having noticed it sooner.

Still, she had to do her due diligence.

Are you…into her, Larry?

She couldn't help but smile as he blushed.

Well, you know. She's very pretty, and man she's funny. I'd just…

She could see the wheels turning in Larry's head. Suddenly, his eyes went wide.

Maybe she could come work with me and Martin! We could use someone to, you know, answer the phones.

Mindy knew this was most likely not the case. Larry had started a new company, which he claimed would revolutionize car warranties, and she knew he could barely afford to pay the electricity bill, but she indulged her little brother.

Couldn't hurt to ask her.

Yea, couldn't hurt to ask…

Larry echoed her words, but she could tell that his mind was already somewhere else:

Wherever Cathy was.

★ ★ ★

And so it was that Cathy came to be the first secretary of the Automobile Protection Corporation, or APCO for short. The first few years at APCO were spent grinding for 18 hours a day as everyone sat around a secondhand mahogany table and chain smoked. It was like a boardroom in drag. Cathy tried to bring some color into the office by buying little bouquets of flowers, but pretty soon, she was doing stuff of real importance, like developing their internal budgeting system. It wasn't easy, though. They took out multiple six-figure loans to stay afloat, but in spite of the challenges, Cathy found herself thoroughly enjoying her work. And they played as hard as they worked.

Every Friday, as soon as 5 o'clock rolled around (or even 4:30, if it'd been a particularly harrowing week), Larry would make them all drinks, transforming the small office into a lively saloon. They did their best to talk about everything but business, usually tuning the radio to 96 Rock and letting Van Halen or Twisted Sister play them into the weekend. Cathy certainly couldn't imagine the CDC having let her drink a grasshopper at work.

One Friday, not long into her time at the company, they were enjoying their weekly bacchanal when the other boys headed out early to happy hour down the street.

No bother, she thought. I'm having a great time with Larry.

So they stayed, and as Larry poured them another round, she noticed his body language shifting. It was at once more anxious and loose. Then she noticed herself beginning to experience something similar, adrenaline coursing through her veins. When Larry handed her the fresh drink, she felt a surge of energy passing between them. The next few minutes passed in a blur. She remembered laughing quite a bit, catching the scent of Larry's natural musk, appreciating its sharp, earthy vitality. And somehow, the two of them kept getting a little closer, and a little closer, and a little closer...

They were both silent, mere inches apart, staring intently into each other's eyes. She could feel the heat of Larry's breath greeting her cheeks, inviting her in. She started to speak without any idea what she might say, but she caught herself. Another long moment passed in which neither said a word. It made the humming of the radio feel distant, like it was on another planet, in some other universe; a universe with no knowledge of Larry's five o'clock shadow, or his soft lips, or his salty musk. It was a universe she wanted nothing to do with, for she felt at this moment that it was impossible to imagine a life lived without him.

Not a second later, they kissed.

It was October 5th, 1984.

★ ★ ★

The next month was a whirlwind. They were head over heels, but they both knew how things might look from the outside. They maintained all prior pretense, presenting themselves to both friends and colleagues as if nothing had changed. Then, on the weekends, they'd drive up to a cabin in the north Georgia mountains, packing a cooler full of champagne and basking in the warm glow of each other's love. They were falling hard, and falling fast.

★ ★ ★

Larry's divorce was made official on December 18th, 1984—one day before Cathy was set to head up to Keene for the Christmas holiday. Larry came with her.

The trip was filled with nervous excitement. Larry had family in Boston at the time, and given that it was Hanukkah, they decided to stop for dinner before doing the final stretch up to Keene. The plan was to enjoy a casual meal with some of Larry's cousins, then meet some of Cathy's brothers at one of Keene's finest dive bars, Phil's.

At dinner, surveying Larry's kin, the trip—and the relationship—suddenly became very real. Cathy was mere hours away from having to face her whole family, to have her actions judged by the Curran tribunal. It was dizzying.

And so she drank. First a glass of champagne. Then another. Then another. And another for good measure. And now that she'd already started, why stop now? So she drank another. And another...

By the time the check was signed, Cathy found herself at the bottom of two bottles of champagne. Larry helped her into the car, and soon, she was sound asleep.

This presented a number of problems for Larry. For starters, how was it going to look if he showed up to meet her brothers for the first time and he presented them with an over-served version of their sister? He could already hear the knuckles cracking. And that was only if he could find the damn guys. He'd only

seen a handful of pictures of them. He wasn't sure he'd even remember what they looked like. But Larry was determined not
to fuck this up. He knew he was falling hard for Cathy, and he
was not ignorant to the fact that they already faced an uphill
battle on the public image front. He resolved to muster all the
affability he could to charm his way into their hearts.

But he wasn't feeling good about his odds.

The bar they were supposed to meet at, Phil's, was exactly
what you'd expect from a small-town watering hole: gravel parking lot, wood facade, neon glow emanating through the windows. Larry sat in the parking lot for a long moment, staring at
Cathy as she snored in the passenger seat. He took a deep breath
and accepted the fact that there was no easy way through. He
reached over and adjusted Cathy into an upright position, placed
one of his jackets on her, and sent up a final prayer to Elohim in
hopes that these Catholic boys would not kick his ass.

Inside, the bar was packed and lively. Strings of tinsel hung
from the rafters. Everyone was smoking. Larry did a cursory
scan of the room, and much to his dismay, immediately spotted
the five Curran boys. The photos hadn't done them justice. In
person, they were even brawnier than he'd imagined. He recognized their faces, but in the heat of the moment, couldn't recall who, exactly, was who. Only one face stood out as instantly
recognizable. Larry could see the photo in his mind's eye. The
man's smile had enraptured him; the fullness of it, the sincer-
ity. It belonged to Tommy, Cathy's closest brother, and it was
on full display this evening.

Larry took a deep breath, tugged at the brim of the rawhide
cowboy hat he'd worn the whole drive up, and sauntered over
to the table.

Tommy Curran?

The Curran men went silent, and five pairs of eyes trained
squarely on Larry. Tommy rose from his stool.

And who are you?

I'm Larry. Larry Dorfman. I came up with Cathy...?

For a brief moment, Tommy said nothing as the wheels turned.

And then he burst into laughter, and suddenly Larry found himself swaddled in a bear hug.

Oh, Larry! How the hell are you? How was the drive?

As Larry laughed, he exhaled sweet relief. Maybe he'd be alright.

Hardly a minute later, they were taking shots and downing beers and trading stories. It was as if Larry had known these men all his life. The conversation flowed with ease. In fact, it was a good half hour before they even thought to ask just where exactly Cathy was. Larry led them out to the car to show them their sister, the sight of which sent all six men into hysterics.

When they slowly roused her, she started with a fright, no doubt mortified to see that Larry had already been fraternizing with her brothers. What stories had been traded? What jokes had been made? What bonds had been made at her expense? It was too much to think about, so she rolled over and went back to sleep. These were all tomorrow's problems.

Much to Cathy's surprise, the rest of the trip went off without a hitch. Celia and Ranger Sr. took to Larry, as did the rest of the family. Larry even helped Ranger chop down a large Christmas tree, and on Christmas Day, as the family drank and discussed plans for next year's white elephant, Larry asked for his name to be thrown into the bowl as well. When he received a slew of odd looks from more than a few Currans seated at the table, he simply smiled and said, Don't worry. I'll be here.

He kept his word. A year later, they were back again. And then again the next year. And the next year. So it went, until one year they returned engaged, and that was that.

They were family. Larry suddenly had nine brothers and sisters. It wasn't long after that they added another member to the family, little Daniel Dorfman, who was instantly taken with his Uncle Tommy. Daniel would spend hours at Tommy's side. They would laugh and play, unconcerned by anything other than the present moment. Cathy and Larry's hearts would swell as they watched the two amuse one another.

Not long after Cathy and Larry got together, Tommy and his fiancée, Chris, moved down to Atlanta. Larry's business was expanding and he hired Tommy to get a new product off the ground. Within a few months, two more Curran men moved down to join the cause, Johnny and Michael. Even young Daniel would come along to the office in a wicker bassinet. Eventually, the hard years turned into not-so-hard years, and then those gave way to great years, and before it was all over, Michael would retire from a 30-year career with EasyCare as the company's chief operating officer.

The universe had other plans for Tommy, though.

In the spring of 1988, he began experiencing severe back pain. He played pickup basketball nearly every day, and Chris and Cathy assumed this was the likely cause of the soreness. But the pain persisted for several weeks, until it got so bad that he could barely stand. Cathy took him to a doc-in-a-box. She was sure it would be a pulled muscle.

It wasn't. Instead, the doctors found five tumors on his lungs, and a severely swollen testicle. That night, he was admitted to Emory Hospital to undergo treatment for cancer.

The next three years were spent in various cycles of joy and grief. No one can ever be prepared for a life-changing diagnosis like cancer, but the family was especially shocked that it had come for Tommy. He was a star-athlete, worked out regularly, and most of all, was a beacon of light. It simply wasn't fair that this was happening to him.

But Tommy was nothing if not a fighter. With consistent treatment, the doctors were able to keep the cancer at bay. He never seemed to miss a beat. There were physical changes, sure. He lost his muscle, and he fatigued quickly. Talking to him, though, he seemed just like the same old Tommy. He was quick-witted, full of jokes that somehow made you feel like you were the most important person in the world, and still overflowing with love for the people around him.

A little over three years into Tommy's battle with cancer, Cathy found herself pregnant. It came as a surprise, and at first, she wasn't sure how she would manage it. No one, however, was more excited to learn of this than Tommy. It invigorated him, gave him another reason to fight, and for a moment, it felt as if things were going to be alright.

Then fate twisted the knife it had stuck into the family's side.

Tommy's health took a turn for the worse. The cancer had become more aggressive, which forced his oncologists at Emory Hospital to start another round of in-patient treatment. Ranger and Celia traveled down from New Hampshire to be with him. A funereal mood settled in as the family anxiously awaited a prognosis.

Roughly five months into her pregnancy, Cathy found the stress almost unbearable. It was like nothing she'd ever experienced before—a feeling beyond worry, beyond fear even, almost a Biblical dread, and it was taking root in her bones. It even seemed to begin manifesting physically. She started experiencing severe abdominal pain and dizziness.

When the aches didn't subside, Cathy's obstetrician ordered a panel of tests. The doctor sat Cathy and Larry down in his office, his lips solemnly pursed.

You have an ovarian cyst. It's very, very likely to be cancerous. We can remove it, but there's a strong chance that we lose the pregnancy. If we don't remove it, it could burst, and you and the baby will almost certainly die, or the cancer could further develop. There's no right choice. It's up to you.

It was too much to process. Too much sadness. Too much death.

Simply too much.

They took the news to Ranger and Celia, who in spite of being devastated, were unequivocal in their response.

You take that cyst out. You can make another baby. We can't make another one of you.

Larry agreed.

Cathy knew they were right. She didn't belabor the point. The next day, she went in for surgery. When Larry squeezed her hand goodbye, he had no idea whether or not she'd be coming back alone. As if the situation weren't terrifying enough, the doctors would not be able to use anesthesia on Cathy for fear of harming the baby, meaning she had to get cut open from abdomen to vagina with only the numbing effects of topical creams and analgesics.

So the surgery proceeded, and Cathy endured with the strength only a woman can muster. They opened her up, pushed the fetus to the side, and removed the problematic ovary. The whole thing took a little over an hour, though to Cathy, it had felt like a lifetime. By the time they stitched her back up, she was too drained of energy to feel anxious about the outcome. The dull tingle of the topical creams was nothing compared to what she felt on the inside.

Your baby's going to be ok.

It took Cathy a second to register the doctor's words. She stared up at the ceiling, experiencing a strange mix of emotions. There was relief, but also confusion, and disbelief, and joy, and grief. They wheeled her back in to see Larry, and they wept in each other's arms. Then they heard the door open.

Congratulations! You did it! You gave birth to a beautiful little ovary!

They turned to find Tommy standing in the door, a bundled-up blanket in his arms.

It's so beautiful. So…bloody. Just gorgeous, Cathy.

They all busted out laughing.

In the following weeks, Cathy did her best to heal from the surgery and prepare to give birth. Over at Emory, Tommy's treatment continued. He was receiving a Hail Mary round of chemotherapy. Throughout it all, even as the Currans began to slowly lose hope for a recovery, Tommy maintained a cheery outlook.

A month before Cathy was due to give birth, she got a call. Larry watched as she took it in bed, saw the look of shock spread across her face, then witnessed the tears begin to spill forth as she hung up.

They're stopping chemo. Tommy is terminal.

It was early April of 1992.

* * *

Larry once again surveyed the dark clouds.

Do you suspect it'll storm? Or just pass over?

The voice was Tommy's, playful as ever, weak though it was. Larry turned around and raised his eyebrows.

I never can tell.

In bed, Cathy stirred.

What an omen.

Larry and Tommy both smiled as Cathy sat up.

As if this baby hasn't already been—

Suddenly, she winced, then looked up, her expression serious.

It's coming.

Within minutes, the medical team had assembled, Larry and Tommy amongst them as Cathy winced and pushed and cried her way toward creation. For all the trouble the pregnancy had been, the actual birth unfolded relatively smoothly. Tommy was even able to help pull the baby out. Cathy looked up just in time to see her brother lifting the newborn aloft, and in the blinding glow of the medical lights, the image took on the air of an angelic vision. In spite of her exhaustion, Cathy smiled.

Hey, Tommy said. This doesn't look like an ovary?

Larry let out a loud boisterous laugh, then turned and steadied himself against the window. Outside, a pocket of blue peeked through the drifting clouds.

★ ★ ★

Two months later, on July 15th, 1992, Thomas Patrick Curran passed away. He smiled until his very last breath. When the Currans laid him to rest in Keene, they were joined by a new pair of curious young eyes. The eyes spent most of their time shut, perhaps to avoid the endless procession of people hoping to look into them. It was for the best, however, that they remained closed, as there was much resting to do.

Tommy Curran's work was now done.

Tommy Dorfman's was just beginning.

THE LOVERS

upright: love, harmony, relationships,
values alignment, choices

reversed: self-love, disharmony, imbalance,
misalignment of values

I take a long drag of my cigarette, surveying my little shrine. The candle has begun to bleed down onto the table. I curse, do my best to try to wipe it off. Shit. Some houseguest I am.

Hands sticky with purple wax, I reach for the next card.

The Lovers.

What a delight. A naked man and woman stand beneath the angel Raphael, its arms outstretched in a gesture of—is it benevolence? Arrogance? Is Raphael serving cunt? I don't know. I've never been much of an expert in this domain. Not that I don't have experience. Frankly, I have too much. Just that I repeat the same mistakes over and over again.

I've heard it said that we learn how to love from our parents, but I find I've learned the most about love from strangers. It was only in fitting to the shape of a foreign body that I began to first find the shape of myself. What I liked, what I didn't like; how I felt, how I didn't feel; what I could give, what I couldn't give. For a long time, I hid behind the veil of a cautious intimacy, "loving" even as I kept the ones I loved at arm's length, never truly knowing them, and them never truly knowing me. Can I really blame myself, though, when my relationship to the carnal began with a lie?

I'm transported back to the spring of 2006, the eternal presence of that moment.

The moment when everything changed.

MYSPACE

I'm not, like, a regular fourteen-year-old or whatever. Like I know I was born in 1992, and yes, it is the year of Our Lord 2006, so I am technically (biologically speaking) fourteen, but a mistake was made, and my spirit, my soul, is at least thirty. My mom has been telling me this for years, "Tommy, you're my little old man!"; "Tommy, you're an *old soul!*"; "Tommy, you're so mature." And because of that I've known since forever that I'm different. More elevated. More sophisticated than most of my peers. That's why I won the "Most Ready for High School" superlative last year in eighth grade. It's just a fact.

Yeah, I like *Gossip Girl* and *The OC* and *Friends* and other basic high school shit, but I also watch *Sex and the City* with my mom and I tried cocaine with my brother like a week ago. I've been drinking since I was twelve, and can be almost moderate enough to not black out each time. I can pour a perfect Ketel One martini with my eyes fucking closed. I go to the mall alone. I have a credit card, or at least numbers to one memorized. I talk to my nanny, Heather, about sex and grown-up shit, because she's basically a friend. Like, I'm just *not* a kid. So yeah, there's basically a thirty-year-old stuck in my bony, pubescent fourteen-year-old body, flexible as it is from all the ballet I do. My hair is flat ironed, bangs sprayed so I can barely see; I wear ripped skinny jeans, Converse, and a Juicy Couture hoodie. I've been out of the closet or whatever for three months now, so I'm thriving.

My taste is superb. While all the boys and girls at my school are still stuck on Abercrombie, I'm already strutting down the halls in American Apparel and vintage YSL, blasting The Killers and Oasis on my pink iPod Mini. Currently, I'm sitting in my bed, scrolling on Xanga, ignoring my best friend Penelope's AIMs, downloading porn on LimeWire for later, and logging into Myspace, where I have like four messages from Laura, my other BFF—and wait. There's another message from someone named Chad Coy?

sup qt?

I can't respond right away because obviously I need to get my FBI on. I click on this complete stranger's profile and— Fuck, he's hot. Hot like out-of-my-league hot. He also like at least ten years older than me, but so what? Age is just a number, and I'm already an old soul, as previously established. So I'm speed-scrolling through his profile, looking at pictures of him drumming shirtless, like in a real fucking band, sweat dripping off his tattooed arms, his hair black and spiky, his ears pierced. Am I about to kiss the drummer of the next Fall Out Boy? A smile that's making my heart race and suddenly I'm hard down there. I keep scrolling through as I touch myself: photos of him and friends, all of them look fucking cool, photos of him smoking cigarettes on balconies I'm already dreaming of being on, in his arms. I stop myself before I get too deep in the fantasy of it all and go back to his message.

Like, is he for real? How did he even find me? I check his Top Eight, and not a familiar face in sight. He's got like twenty thousand friends, and we don't have any mutuals. I reach for my mouse, realizing my hands are clammy and wet. I feel nauseated trying to come up with a response. Like, he's clearly older, which means he probably wants sex, because that's what all older guys want, right? Every episode of *SATC* ever has made that clear. And I still haven't had sex with a guy before. I mean, I'm not a virgin or anything, Vallerie Mitchell took my v-card in seventh grade. But I haven't had a lot of experiences with dudes. Mark, the first guy I did anything with, well...we only sucked each other off.

I check Chad's age: twenty-seven. Okay, that's like, whatever, my parents have a big age gap and yeah, like I said I'm fourteen, but not like really. He's twice my age, which means twice my experience, but I'm overthinking it. Things with Mark aren't going to go any further, and there's literally no other gay guys— at least out and cute—at school so it's time to date a real man anyway. Plus, I'm already in love, even without meeting him. He's the one. Fuck it, I'm gonna respond.

nm. jc. Dinner soon probs. you?

Before I can even stress about it he responds.

Chad: cool. Ur mad cute btw.

tommy: u2

Chad: thx

tommy: :)

Chad: we should meet sometime

I'm gonna puke. This is insane. He's so sweet and hot and

like…ugh, I'm already speechless. I can't wait to tell Penelope and Laura tomorrow at school.

tommy: yah, that sounds cool.

Chad: cool. tm?

tommy: as in like tomorrow?

Chad: rofl yaaaaa

tommy: aight. sure. txt me

My pink Razor phone vibrated in my back pocket. I scramble to get it out of my jeans and open it. He texted me so quickly, a backward smiley face. I save his number and respond.

tommy: I'll let you know about tomorrow

Chad: Cool I can pick you up whenever.

tommy: <3 k

I scream into my pillow and notice I'm still hard. I close my eyes and think of his muscles, his lips, his hair, and start jacking off. I cum in my jeans and I don't fucking care. I change into sweats, speedily, grab a cigarette from my desk drawer, and climb out the window to smoke in the dewy Atlanta air.

I imagine the heat is muggy with his sweat.

★ ★ ★

This seems…strange? Why does this grown-up want to hang out with you, Penelope asks. *Like…*

We're lying on her bedroom floor, carpet prickling into our backs, staring up at leftover glow-in-the-dark sticky stars that have lost their light. I look to the right and see Chad Michael Murray's gorgeous face. It smells like her mother's cooking meatballs downstairs, Avril Lavigne is playing from her bedside radio on 94.1. She has a cute pink swivel chair I desperately want, and the gumball machine I gave her for Valentine's Day in sixth grade is collecting dust on her desk. Our bellies are full from all the ripe red cherries I had left over from lunch. I was too excited to eat then.

I turn on my side to face her. *There's chemistry, P. I know it doesn't make sense but he's so sweet. He's…*

I want to end the statement with…*burrowed his way into my heart, he's already mine*, but all I can muster is, *He's cool. I swear.*

Her freckled nose scrunches up into tiny little wrinkles, as if I'd farted, *But that's gross, dude, like find someone—*

THERE ISN'T ANYONE, I snap back. *Ugh, sorry, just like… you're not gay, okay? You don't get it. There like just…there isn't anyone else. And finally, after Mark, somebody thinks I'm cute, we have, like, similar interests. And it doesn't feel weird or whatever like I hang out with my twenty-eight-year-old brother all the time and my cousins. It's not like he's sixty.*

She laughs at this. *Okay, I guess I see your point…*

I can see in her eyes that she doesn't mean this, but she's trying to be supportive. I just want love; I want to be loved, I want someone to pay attention to me, and Chad is doing that. What does Penelope know about grown-up love anyway? I don't need her approval.

Cool… I put my hand on her heart and lean my forehead against hers. I need her to hear me now.

Just…if you could be, like, happy for me and support me in this, that would really be cool.

She nods her head against mine, red bangs scratching my nose. She breaks, standing up, almost excited.

So! When are you supposed to see him?! she asks, grabbing a cherry from her bedside table.

Well. Tonight? I mean, I dunno. I just. I felt weird telling Heather about it because she like always wants to ask question after question and it's just...

I make a throw-up face. Heather's been my nanny for years, and even though she likes to tell me about her love life and dating drama, I kind of keep this part of myself hidden from her.

But now I need to fully let Penelope in on the whole secret.

He's...um...picking me up in like thirty.

Wait—he's coming here?! Penelope swiftly turns to me.

Just to pick me up!

Oh my fucking GOD! Tommy!

I can see Penelope formulating a rebuttal, but I'm not going to let her have it. I have to see Chad tonight—there's no other way—it means more to me than anything else. I'd rather fucking die, so I keep talking.

He's not like coming in or anything—you don't even have to lie! He's gonna pick me up and drive me home. He'll drop me off and Heather will think it was you, and you can tell your parents Heather came to get me. Nbd!

Penelope gives me a look, and it's the epitome of a ¯_(ツ)_/¯ emoji. But I know that I convinced her, and she won't fight back. Not at this point. I win 99 percent of the time. It's just, like, the dynamic of our relationship.

Fine, she says. *Just have him go far, like way far, down the street. And don't do anything stupid. Please.*

I jump up and hug her, gripping her so hard we both fall onto her bed laughing away her fears of—and for—me.

★ ★ ★

April in Atlanta means rain, which means sticky grass clinging to my sneakers. It means streetlamps glowing on slick wet pavement. It means bugs I can't identify nipping at my ankles and screaming so incessantly in the night that you forget they're even there. Some nights, it haunts me. Tonight, it feels romantic. I used the last of Penelope's hair spray to glue my bangs down and more than a touch of her Clinique Happy perfume to freshen up. As I stand on the street, several houses down from Penelope's, my throat feels dry, my lips feel chapped, my cheeks feel flushed. I can't stop opening and closing my phone—*click click*—and licking my lips as I look right, left, right again. A few cars pass by, and I think it might be him. Then I see a black Honda Civic cruise up, and I get a glimpse of a jawline I could never mistake, and I think he's decided I'm not cute enough, until he turns around and pulls up right in front of me. Fall Out Boy is blasting from his radio and he yells over it, "Hey you. Wanna ride?"

The car is terrifying. It has an actual stick shift and is easily older than me. The seats smell like moldy English breakfast tea. My feet are swallowed up by empty chip bags and Gatorade bottles. I'm trembling, nervous, but not scared. I can't be scared. I'm grown.

Hey, I say, stealing a glance at him beneath my bangs. I feel like a Sim character. Like can I even speak English anymore? The word *hey* felt foreign coming out of my mouth, like I'm hearing my voice for the first time, and now I'm embarrassed, like is that how I sound.

So, what do you want to do? he asks, flashing a smile. I decide to make eye contact with him, to be grown.

Um... I don't—I mean, we could—

My words are stumbling out of my mouth, I take a deep breath. Get your shit together, Tommy! I try again, this time more chill.

I'm really open. Like whatever you think. We could see a movie or something? As soon as the words come out of my mouth, I feel a wave of regret. Is this even a date? I have no idea.

Oh, for sure. That sounds cool. Yeah, let's. He slams his foot on the gas pedal, peels back out into the road. I feel fully at the mercy of this way too hot stranger driving like a fucking maniac from Druid Hills to a theater in Atlantic Station. But I won't dare ask him to slow down.

He buys the movie tickets. Did we even discuss what we were seeing? I'm just enthralled with him, the pulsing of his veiny arms. He walks slightly ahead of me into the theater and we take our seats.

My heart is pounding like a fucking river dancer, each beat resonating through every atom of my tiny frame. Before I can slow down and take a sip of the Coke he bought me, his knee touches mine. His hand follows and he rests it on my thigh. Like a magnet, my hand locks to his. I brave another glance, and he's already staring at me. That smile again. My whole body is hard, desperate for him to kiss me.

I think he can tell. And he makes me wait for it. We stay like that, almost frozen, the whole movie.

We speed-walk out of the theater, under fluorescent garage lights. I feel electric, and he does, too. I can tell.

I have a place in mind, he says. *If you wanna go somewhere else for a minute? I mean, I'd like to.*

I check my phone. 9:48 p.m. I have to be home soon, but I don't want this to end—whatever *this* is. I nod. *Yeah.* He smirks again.

Cool.

We drive off in silence, passing shops and restaurants as they're closing up. I see people getting in their cars, driving safely home, probably to their families, to somewhere tamer and far less interesting than the passenger seat of Chad's car.

Finally, he pulls into an empty unlit lot in Piedmont Park.

Have you ever walked through the park at night?

No. I chuckle. *I haven't had that death wish.*

He laughs at my joke. *It's safe, I promise.*

And in light of everything I've ever been taught about stranger danger or keeping my wits about me from my parents, not to mention all the movies I've seen where I'd be screaming at myself through the screen—*Don't do it! You fucking idiot! It's so obvious!*—I somehow trust him.

He hops out of the car, and before I can open my door, he's opening it for me. *What a gentleman.* I follow him. I mean, he could tell me that we're here on a mission to murder stray kittens, and I would still follow him. I feel tethered to him now.

Chad clearly isn't a teenager. He isn't dorky or stupid or in a hurry to rush home to his mama. He doesn't worry about homework or making good grades. He's in a fucking band and he has his own car, his own apartment. He's a man. He's my man. He knows what he's doing, and I will do anything for him.

Chad jumps a small fence into the park. I fumble after him and fall to my knees. He helps me back up and pulls me along, further into the darkness of the empty park, and his hand finds its way around my waist. He stops abruptly, I look up and before I can say anything he kisses me. I swear I'm levitating at this point, he has me pressed against him. I've never been in the arms of someone this strong before, and it feels right, like exactly where I'm supposed to be. His tongue is smooth, and his kisses are slow but forceful. He breaks, laughing a little. Suddenly I feel grown, devilish even. Mischievous. He walks me deeper into the unknown spaces of the park, stopping every few yards to kiss me. I mean, I've been to this park a hundred thousand times, but always in the light of day. Right now, it's another world. We make our way to the edge of a small pond, surrounded by trees and bushes, but not another human in sight, because it's nighttime (obviously).

Chad sits down on a bench and pulls me into his chest. I'm awkward standing over him, but we're kissing and it feels good. His lips are harder than any lips I've kissed, and his stubble is scratching my face. I've never known what that feels like. Now I do. And I want more of it. His confidence, or maturity, or whatever it is—it's intoxicating. He pulls my hips against his mouth and starts kissing my belly. He takes my shirt off, and then my pants. I don't have anything to say, it's all just instinct at this point. Feeling nearly naked in my blue-and-white-striped underwear in the middle of Piedmont Park. Feeling alive. He starts kissing my thighs and slides my underwear down to my ankles.

I've never been naked like this outside. It seems wrong, but Chad seems right. My mind is racing. *What if we get caught? What if we get arrested? What if—* And before I can finish that thought, he has me inside his mouth, and I've fully submitted. The night air is like a flame against my back, pushing me even closer to him, the trees our only witnesses. He stops, looks up at me.

You're so fucking clean. You have like no hair, anywhere, he says, smiling.

It's true. I don't.

I'm sorry, I say softly.

No. It's hot. It's a good thing.

And he slowly pushed me back inside his mouth. I came almost immediately and he swallowed it. He undid his belt and then wiggled his skinny jeans down. I could see his dick, hard in his white Hanes underwear. It looked smaller than Mark's, but not, like, *small* small.

I kiss him up and down his neck and broad chest, and breathe in his Axe body spray, and I'm filled with some strange confidence I've never felt before. I lick right above the band of his underwear, right and left, and he pulls them down. I'm on my knees now, and I start sucking him off. I feel his hand on my head, petting me. His other hand slides down my back and grabs my ass. He removes it, and I can hear him spit, maybe, but I can't quite tell, because his dick tastes like iron, and I'm trying to pretend I don't have pubes getting lodged in the back of my throat.

I feel his hand again, on my lower back. He slides it between my cheeks and his finger starts playing with my hole.

I move to get off his dick and he pushes me back down and I smack his hand away. He lets me go.

Whoa, I say.

Everything okay?

Yeah, I just— What were you doing down there? My confidence wavers, and I don't want to sound naive, but I'm too shocked not to ask.

Oh, you'll like it. I promise.

I can tell he means that, which means it must be true. I lay my cheek on his belly, stroke his dick, and he starts playing with my hole again. Suddenly, his finger jams into my body, and my jaw clenches. My body feels cold all of a sudden, like a thousand times more sensitive than it was before, and I don't know if I like this feeling or not. I let out a little cry.

Just breathe, he says, but there's an intensity, an edge, a fire to his voice. I don't want to disappoint him, so I obey. I try to breathe; I try to relax into it, but I'm failing. What was pleasurable seems to be turning into something else. Still, I don't want to say no to him. I'm no longer enjoying this, yet he seems to be enjoying it more and more. And maybe that's what adult sex is, and all that matters to me right now is that—more than my own pleasure, my own feelings of safety or security—I want him to feel good and be impressed by my adultness. I don't want him to be mad at me or leave me. So I stroke him while he fingers me, and I keep stroking him until right before he cums, and he sticks his dick so deep in my throat that tears are running down my cheeks, and I've never tasted someone else's cum before, and I don't like it, but I somehow manage to swallow. When he's done, he lowers himself down to the ground and starts kissing me, sweetly.

Wasn't that good, boy?

Boy? Is that how he sees me? I don't like the thought of that. We're lovers. We're two mature people making like an informed, adult choice. Together. Right? Right.

Yeah, that was...

I'm not sure if it was or wasn't, so I just don't say anything, and I keep smiling. He stands up, puts his pants on, and helps me get dressed. I'm shivering, I don't know why. He takes the light coat he has and puts it over my shoulders. It smells of stale cigarettes. Then he pulls out a pack of them, fingers one out, tosses it in his mouth. Lights it and takes a long drag. He hands it to me, and we share it as we walk back to his car. I feel dizzy from the nicotine. In spite of everything, I feel accomplished.

I tried a new thing.

★ ★ ★

Sitting in first period Spanish, I can't stop replaying last night's events over and over in my head. Jessica, my teacher (we call them by their first names at my hippie-dippie school) is prepping the board for some lesson or another, and I can hear murmurs of people in my class talking, but everything sounds like gibberish, because I'm playing the tape of last night in my head, and if I close my eyes, I can almost taste him again. I mean, I did things that I couldn't have imagined doing. I feel like I grew up in a single night. Penelope plops down next to me at the shared table.

So how was it?

I run her through the whole night in a whisper. Her face is held frozen until I finish. Then she shrugs her shoulders and sighs, averts her eyes.

That sounds kind of scary, T.

I feel crushed. How does my best friend not get it? How could she not see how mature I'd been in handling everything? What upsets me the most, though—and I don't think I'm even aware of this fact—is the fear that she might be right.

Can you not be happy for me? I feel like I grew up in the course of the last twelve hours and left her in the dust somewhere.

I can always be happy for you. It's just this particular thing, I don't know. You're right. I'm sorry, like, that's cool. I am happy for you.

Okay, I say. *Thank you.*

Jessica starts blabbing to us in Spanish, something about a test coming up, and my mind starts to wander back to that nagging fear: *Was* it as gross as Penelope thought it was? Sure, the whole thing had been a lot at once. I can see that. And on some level, there was an element of fear, but I think that's how it's supposed to be. It's supposed to feel weird. Anything worth doing is going to make you feel a little tingly. But my mind won't rest. I need to take control of this. So I text him from under the table.

Tommy: that was fun

Chad: yeah, boy. Ur rly hot.

tommy: u2.

Chad: what r u up to thurs?

tommy: nm

Chad: cool. We should chill.

tommy: aight. Lmk.

Thank God. He likes me. He wants to see me again. That's all that matters now. I'm crawling out of my skin. I can't focus. I wanna throw my notebook across the room and exclaim *I'M IN LOVE* and storm out belting "My Junk" from *Spring Awakening*. And then I remember it's only Tuesday.

How the FUCK am I going to wait that long?

★ ★ ★

Every noise I make tiptoeing down the hall, past my parents' bedroom—their sound machine rumbling behind the door—and down the forest green carpeted stairs feels infinitely louder than it probably is. I check my phone. It's 12:15 a.m. Chad's latest message is still up on the screen.

I'm outside.

I make my way through the yard and to the back gate. I'm skinny enough to slide through it, but I spot the motion detector, which will shine bright if I engage it. After a moment's consideration, I decide the safest bet is to spider-crawl down my steep driveway. After what feels like forever, I make it to the street.

I open the passenger door and immediately jump on Chad. We make out for a minute. It's ferocious, animalistic. He puts the car in Drive, and after we're a few houses away, he turns up the Fall Out Boy CD he's got on deck and speeds off.

So where now? I ask him.

Mine?

Cool, I say, remembering to put my seat belt on as we turn onto the freeway. The bottles and trash covering the floor don't bother me now. I just brush them aside like leaves.

We arrive at a terrifying-under-any-other-circumstance beige building. He holds my hand up three flights of stained carpeted stairs, down a gray hallway with fluorescent lights, stopping only to unlock his apartment door.

Inside the apartment is dark and smells sour. Dishes are piled up in the sink, there's literally a few flies licking plates clean, and clothes are scattered across the beige, scratchy carpeted living room floor. The furniture is simple: a shabby plaid couch, fraying Lay-Z-Boy, and what appear to be lawn chairs. There's a small coffee table with an ashtray full of cigarette butts and a dirty bong. But before I can even get grossed out, the door closes behind me and I feel Chad's arms wrap around my waist. He kisses my left ear, biting on it a little, which I like apparently, then moves to my neck and slides his hand up my shirt.

Do you want a beer or anything? he asks.

Sure, I whisper. I don't really like beer. I'm more of a hard liquor, swig from a bottle of Jack Daniel's–type, but whatever. He hands me a room-temp Natty Light, and I take a sip. The liquid fizzes down my throat, and before I can take another sip, his tongue is in my mouth, whirling around like one of the rides at

Lemonade Days, a festival up in Dunwoody that I used to go to as a kid. He lifts me up with ease, placing me onto the counter and spreading my legs. He strips my shirt off and gives me tiny kisses down the chiseled contours of my ballet-toned belly. I lean back onto my forearms, anticipating what's to come next, closing my eyes, biting my lips. Fingers move below my waistline, and the button on my jeans pops open. I can feel the zipper slowly releasing, the metal cold against my dick. He lifts my hips up and slides my pants right off. The cold counter tile, combined with Chad's tongue grazing my inner thigh, sends shivers up and down my spine. My skin breaks out in goose bumps. His shadow covers me, and he whispers in my ear, *This way*, before lifting me upright and setting me back down on the ground.

He slowly leads me to the living room, then he abruptly stops me, slides my underwear off, sits me down on one of the green-and-blue-plaid lawn chairs. Without a second thought, he starts slowly sucking me off, gently working his way downward, ultimately licking my balls, which tickles. He lifts my knees up above my head, looks at me with a mischievous grin. I smile back, because I can tell my flexibility is exciting to him. Then his lips meet my thighs, and he traces tiny kisses around my crotch. *Is this what teasing feels like?* I wonder. Suddenly, his tongue moves from my sack to that area of soft supple skin between my balls and my ass. He stays here for a while, doing figure eights with his tongue, and I feel almost sick with pleasure. I rest my hand on his spiky hair and he pushes my legs further back, his tongue sliding down and—

Whoa, I don't know what he's doing anymore.

Uhhhhhhhhhh— I try to get a word out through giggles. Whatever he's doing down there, with his mouth, tickles. He just moans. His palms spread my butt cheeks apart and he goes deeper with his tongue, more intricate variations, like he's writing me a love letter. I'm reeling now, my whole body feels numb. I don't even have words for sensations like this. I could almost puke, and before I do, I explode warm liquid onto my chest, my chin, I see it fly past my head, and I deflate into a blob of a human. I feel high. My legs rest on his shoulders and I can feel his mouth sucking up drops of me as he makes his way to my mouth. I don't like the taste of my own cum, but I can't form a sentence to make it stop.

He stands over me and presses his dick into my mouth. I run my left hand up his happy trail and squeeze his chest, my right pushes against his hip, I'm choking on it, but realize I can breathe through my nose. The tip of his dick pushes against my throat and I'm gagging, but I like it. Quickly he pulls out and smacks my cheeks with it, jacking himself off, until his liquid sprays all over my face. It's hot. Sticky. Dripping. I'm too shocked to move, pinching my eyes closed tightly because I don't want it to get in there. I hear him walk away and come back, a towel presses against my face and he cleans me up.

Damn baby, I got you good, he says.

Yeah, I whisper back.

You alright?

Mmm-hmm.

Your ass is so clean.

Thanks, I say, smiling, sitting up. I reach for my underwear. I stand up and find my jeans, pulling my phone out of the pocket. It's nearly three in the morning. "Fuck, I need to head back."

"For sure," he says, walking over to me. We lock eyes. "You're really fucking beautiful, Tommy," He kisses me again, softer this time.

Chad drops me off at my house. I sneak back in, quietly, tip-toeing on the marble floors with my sneakers clutched tightly in my right hand. My ass still feels wet from his mouth, and my heart pounds through my chest. I'm so lightheaded that I have to stop myself at the bottom of the staircase. *Am I moving, like, way too quickly?* Just then, my family's bulldog snorts, jolting me back to the present.

Shh, Bailey, I whisper, walking over to pet her on the head. *Good girl.*

I press my forehead against hers, and her tongue grazes my nose. When I wipe her slobber off my upper lip, I can still smell Chad on my fingers. I inhale him again, and my body shivers.

Maybe I'm really grown now.

My heart won't stop beating. What am I supposed to do? Does everyone feel like this after sex? Was this even sex? This feels like excitement—or is it fear? Behind me, my parents' bar beckons. As quietly as I can, I unscrew the cap on my mother's Ketel One (her favorite) and take a long swig. It burns at first, but then the warmth spreads throughout my insides, and I feel like I'm back in my body again.

Upstairs in my room, I strip down into my underwear, put a *Sex and the City* tape in my TV, and tuck myself in.

Am I a Samantha? I giggle to myself.

Maybe I am.

★ ★ ★

Tommy, wake up kiddo you're—Jesus—you're already late little dude. My nanny Heather's voice jolts me awake.

Fuck.

I'M UP. Just getting dressed.

Why is your door locked?

I don't remember doing that. I try not to sound flustered.

Mistake I guess or whatever. Give me a second. I'll be down in five.

I run to my sink and splash my face with water and catch my reflection. I look older I think, like I somehow aged five years in the last twelve hours.

Heather is waiting for me in the kitchen, black plastic sunglasses damming up her bangs and preventing them from spilling over her eyes, which they often like to do.

Where are Mom and Dad? I ask, slinging my torn Jack Spade messenger bag over my right shoulder.

They flew out this morning. Daniel is coming down to stay with you this weekend.

G too?

Nope just D.

Gotchya. Uh, can we like stop at Starbucks?

Fat chance, kiddo.

My eyes roll so far back into my head I can see my brain. She just scoffs, turns on her heels, and walks away.

Daniel is my older brother by four and half years, and my only full sibling. He's currently a freshman at USC. Not fancy Los Angeles USC, armpit-of-the-South-frat-bro-Columbia–South Carolina USC. G, my adopted brother, is four days younger than Daniel, and goes there as well. They were best friends growing up, and G was *always* over at our house. At some point, he just never left. I have two half siblings that are older than them, but they feel more like my aunt and uncle, they're like full-on adults at this point, eleven and fourteen years older than me I rarely see them.

School is a blur. I wanna tell Laura and Penelope about Chad and last night, but I don't think they'd get it. They've never gone past first base, and I hit a home run with Vallerie in the seventh grade. I hadn't even jacked off yet. I had no idea what was going on, but we did it. Somehow. If you can call it "it." But now I *really* know what "it" is. And whatever I did with Vallerie…that wasn't it, babes.

I'm so tired and out of it by fourth period that I almost fall asleep on the clay pot I spun for art class. In fifth period—free period—I walk over to the park across from school and smoke a cigarette. I want to text Chad, but I don't know what to say.

By the time I get home, Daniel and his friends are already partying hard.

Fuck, buddy. Where you been?!

My brother embraces me with that kind of hug only a drunk straight boy can give and I nearly suffocate.

School, dude. My voice drops like five octaves when I talk to him. I wanna be more myself, but also his straight friends kinda scare me, so I feel like I need to reel it in a bit.

Tight, tight. Yo, you wanna beer?

Vodka?

Straight for the hard shit, I like it. Take it easy though, k?

I walk to the counter and pour myself a shot and down it, no chaser.

He pats me on the back.

Suddenly, I'm awake again. I take another shot and go talk to his girlfriend, Shelly. She has thin blond hair and desperate blue eyes. I feel like I can be more myself around her.

You want a bump? She asks me, giggling in my ear.

What?

Like, you wanna bump of blow? She smirks. I hesitate.

She grabs my wrist and drags me into the bathroom. Fishing around in her low-rise jean pocket, she comes back up with a baggie and a key, then scoops up a chunk of the white powder and puts it in my face.

I lower my head to meet the key with my right nostril.

Yeah, then cover the left, she says. I do, and it burns, but then a numbness starts spreading down the back of my throat. I cough and laugh and ask her for another.

Don't tell your brother, she says. *God I love you!!!*

Duh, love you too bitch! And we walk out arm in arm, all giggly and coked out.

Friday's aren't usually this crazy this early, but when D's in town, I never know what to expect. The night rolls on, and cigarette after cigarette, I find myself more engaging and funny and attractive than I've ever been. And it's weird I can drink more and not get as drunk. *I like this.*

Around two thirty, most of D's friends have bounced, and he and Shelly are half–passed out on the sofa. I decide to lie down in my parents' room, because their TV gets cable and I'm not tired enough to fall asleep.

Chad. I remember. It's funny how life can just sweep me up sometimes, and I get so caught up in a moment and I forget about everything else. But the thought of him makes me excited. I grab my phone and text him. Before I can even put it back down it vibrates.

Chad: should I come ov?

tommy: do you want to?

Chad: What are you wearing right now?

tommy: Just my underwear... ;)

That's a lie, I still have my shoes and ripped skinnies and this big cardigan I grabbed from my grandfather's closet in New Hampshire on. I wished I had more of my brother's coke, but it's too late now. I jump from the bed and strip my clothes off in front of their full-length mirror. I see my legs, bare and bony, knees jutting out, and I touch myself to get my dick somewhat hard and snap a few pics, trying to get the right angle. Biting my lower lip, I stare at my reflection. *You can do this.*

I hit Send.

Chad: fuckkkkk, I'm cumming over

tommy: yay! okay. Just like be quiet though lmk when ur here and I'll come get you.

Thirty minutes pass and it feels like a lifetime. I don't even know what to do with myself. I check AIM and nobody is awake. I start scrolling on Myspace and—

Buzz

My phone goes off on the nightstand. I throw my T-shirt back on, tiptoe over frat boys to the front door. He's already there when I open it, and I put my finger on his mouth *shh*, leading him in, by his hand, into my parents' bedroom.

Before I can lock the door, he's ripping my shirt off. He pulls my head back, his tongue slides in my ear. It tickles in a good way. I kiss him, imitating a passion I've memorized from a thousand viewings of *The Notebook*. He reeks of booze and cigarettes, and I love it. He throws me on the bed, so hard I have to catch my breath, but before I even get the chance, he's on top of me, he flips me over, playing my ear again like an instrument with his tongue. Then he makes a zigzag with his saliva, like a snail, all the way down my back, to my ass, spreading my cheeks. I have to bite into the pillow to keep from screaming. He comes back up for air, grinds his hard dick against my bare ass.

I wanna fuck you so bad, boy, he whispers in my ear.

Uh-huh, is all I can muster. I'm not sure what he means. Aren't we fucking already?

Before I can ask more questions he's off me, rummaging around in the pockets of his jeans. He pulls out a condom, smiles. He slides it on his dick, never breaking eye contact. I can't look away; it's too piercing. It's as if he's looking right through me. This doesn't feel right, but I don't know how to say that. Plus, I'm drunk. My mouth won't work. He comes back onto the bed, grabs my ankles, spreads my legs, and slides my body toward his. The rubber squeaks as it rubs against my skin, and he presses his forehead against mine, pulls back and spits into his hand, continues to look right through me. *What is he doing?*

Then he rubs his spit down there, between my cheeks, and slides a finger in. A pit forms in my stomach.

Um...

I try to say something, to form words, to come up with a

coherent argument as to why this shouldn't be happening right now. But it doesn't come.

Shhh. He kisses me again.

I try again to speak, but he keeps kissing me, his tongue lodging itself in my throat, working its way further and further down.

I manage to get out, *I don't—*

But what don't I? I don't know anymore what I do or what I don't. I want him and the way he smells, but I'm shaking and my heart is pounding. Maybe it's the coke. Something doesn't feel right.

Chad pulls his fingers out of my ass and positions the tip of his dick against my hole.

I've wanted this since I first saw you, he says.

I don't know what you're doing, I reply.

Just breathe.

And I try that. I didn't even know I'd been holding my breath. *You can do this whatever this is going to be. You're grown. You can do it.*

He pushes the tip of himself into me, and I clench my jaw. I want to push him off, but I can't move. I'm cock-stunned. Frozen. I see my own ankles and feet resting on his shoulders, and wonder how they got there in the first place. *Are those feet even my feet?* His stale breath starts to feel suffocating.

Ow.

Just breathe, baby. You're doing great.

No, this hurts, I finally say.

It won't in a minute, if you just relax.

Okay, relax, I tell myself. *Just. Relax.*

And I try. I want to be good. I want him to be happy. I don't want him to hate me. He pushes deeper inside me, and fuck it hurts, it burns with a harsh, unrelenting stingy burn, feels like he's pressing into my stomach.

Is he ripping me apart?

There you go, just like that, baby, he says. *Fuck, you're so fucking tight baby. You're so fucking tight.* He kisses my neck, his whole body on top of me.

I look down and see my dick is soft. I can feel my cheeks flushing. *Fuck, this is embarrassing.* I stare back up at him, his head is pointed upward, eyes closed. Droplets of sweat move down from his hairline. I stare past him up to the ceiling fan, and do that thing where I focus on one of the fan's arms and follow it around and around and around again until the fan slows down. He's pushing into me, but I can't even feel it anymore, all I can see is the fan going around and around. My head lightly taps the headboard, and his breathing is getting faster, but I can only see the fan going around and around. Then he falls on me and I snap back to him, his sweaty hot body laid against my own, which is not hot, not even warm, but a cold shell. He pulls out, and I'm trembling. I can't move though; I feel paralyzed. *Thank God this is over*, I think. He turns me around. In front of me, I see a photo of my parents on my father's bedside table, and suddenly he reenters me. I bite down on the pillow in front of me as hard as I can.

This is what you wanted, right, baby? he asks, whispering into my left ear.

Uh. Is that all I can fucking say? *Uh, uh, uh.* Maybe it is what I wanted? Or want? I don't even know anymore. I asked him to come over, so yes. I guess so? But if it's what I want, why do I feel tears streaming down my face right now—why do I feel disgusting? Why do I want to disappear? Why does his breath feel like it's burning a hole into the back of my neck as he pumps faster and faster, moving at a hundred miles per hour inside of me, until he stiffens up too? He cums, I suppose. Then he plops down, raises his hips ever so slightly, and pulls out for a final time I hope. I hear the condom pop off, and it flies over my head, landing on the bedside table in front of me, filled with his cum.

Fuck, he says, with a laugh. *You're amazing.*

I can't respond.

I should probably go before—

Yeah. Wouldn't want my parents to find us. And I laugh, too. I want to make light of this situation somehow. Make him feel like it was all okay.

He excitedly hops out of bed, and I watch as he dresses.

See you soon, kiddo, he says before kissing my forehead and walking out the door.

My ass burns. I can't get out of this bed. But I need to. I need to inspect myself. I feel wet and gross down there, like maybe there's blood. I check. There isn't. Then I get up, and I take a long look at myself in the mirror.

You did it. You should be proud. That was a good thing. A cool thing. You're hot. Boys want to fuck you. You did it.

You're grown.

And then I wince.

THE SHOPBOY

I must've been, what, fifteen? Riding down the escalator at Neiman Marcus in Atlanta, I locked eyes with a dapper, bespectacled boy who looked to be only a few years older than me. His silver name tag read Freddie—a name befitting his soft, handsome face. I could tell by the greased coif of his hair that I had a chance. *Gay!*

He was making his way up to the second floor with a handful of conservative trousers. I looked at them, then straight into his eyes, and we held each other's gaze until we slowly but surely passed. When he reached the top of the escalator, he immediately turned and followed me. Back then, I had a way with men, a confidence that approached a kind of carnal mysticism. I could pull a man in with the flick of an eye, invariably feel their gaze bearing down on my back, their breath as they approached me. Such is the ignorant bliss of youth.

Freddie was no exception. I felt the warm touch of his whisper before I even turned around.

Are you finding everything okay?

I turned slightly.

Actually, could you show me where the Tom Ford section is?

Tom Ford had recently launched his eponymous label and I'd seen an editorial in some fashion magazine at Borders with these tiny swimsuits and, frankly, cannon *Simple Life* oversized glasses. Summer was around the corner and I needed a bathing suit that would show off my ass in all the right ways. I'd had my eyes on a black classic short that Mr. Ford had recently released, which hugged my hips and sat just above my teenage bulge, with a waistband and little belt that emphasized the taper of my V-shaped abdomen. I was at once fit and frail. A true ballet dancer's physique. I didn't appreciate it enough.

Growing up, Tom Ford was like the Pope to me. I combed through all his editorials, read all his blogs, studied all his fashion shows. Studying his time at Gucci was a formative experience for me, and I would spend hours in the mall in late elementary and early middle school talking to managers and shopgirls at luxury stores. It's not like I was buying anything, just devoted to collecting lookbooks and fragrance samples. Gucci was always my first stop at Phipps Plaza, then the Valentino Boutique, followed by Jeffrey, but it took a village to cultivate my sartorial tastes and budding shopping addiction. Barney's Co-Op across the way actually tracked my height with a pencil in one of the dressing rooms as I was still growing. I think they all felt sorry for me, amused by my curiosity and desire to try anything—and everything—on. Were I growing up now, I would be, like, TikTok famous or something, and probably would crash and burn by thirteen. Thank God I was born pre-unboxing-era because I would never forgive myself.

But back to Freddie. He raised an eyebrow at me, then spoke in a tone that was both sensual and hurried. He was nervous:

This way.

As we walked, he trailed a few centimeters behind me, like he was ushering me into a secret section—*our* section. The tension was palpable. I had my head cocked ever so slightly, keeping the faintest of eyes on him as I tried to anticipate his path. When we got to the Tom Ford section, I instantly spotted the shorts I was looking for, but I pretended to browse while Freddie asked me dumb questions about school and my family.

Yawn. Do better, Freddie.

He was hot, what with his repressed prep school vibe.

Finally, I grabbed the swimsuit, ready to move onto the next stage of this hidden-in-plain-sight courtship. He eyed the piece.

Excellent choice.

Freddie turned and led me to a fitting room, and when he opened the door, I felt a surge of electricity coursing through me. There was a pregnant pause as we both stood in the doorway. I could tell I was putting him through hell. Finally, I entered, feigned like I was pulling the door shut—and then left it cracked, curious as to what I could get away with.

Pretending to not feel his eyes on me, I undressed and slid into the suit's tight black fabric. I surveyed myself in the mirror, ensuring the look was right, then finally turned over my left shoulder to greet him.

Made for you, I think.

Really?

Really.

I gave him a coy smile.

Okay, I'll take it. And with that, I abruptly shut the door, and it felt like all the air in my body *whooshed* out at once. My veins were on fire, I was coursing with adrenaline. Fuck, that was hot.

At the cash register, I recited my mom's credit card number from memory, and I could tell this set Freddie's aspirational heart even more a flutter. This wasn't anything particularly remarkable. I'd become reliant on spending my parents' money; it felt like the only way to get them to pay attention to me was via a bank statement. Growing up against the backdrop of Nicole, Blair, and Serena, and *My Super Sweet 16* with an immense amount of privilege and a highly addictive personality type meant that I gravitated to the Atlanta luxury retail scene.

I watched as Freddie meticulously folded the bathing suit, wrapping it in white tissue and sensually placing it into the notorious Neiman Marcus silver bag. I slid down the Prada Sport sunglasses that were resting on top of my head, using them to shield my eyes lest he see how googly they'd gone.

Thanks, I said through a smirk, then turned on my heels and walked away, feeling his eyes track me all the way up the escalator. I walked to the car on cloud fucking nine, and when I peeked into the bag I saw the corner of a crisp business card with his name and cell phone number written on the back. Without a second thought, I texted him.

Hi. My go to.

Hello was formal and robotic, *hey* was for friends, and *hi* translated to *I want you to eat my ass for five hours after a skinny sushi dinner date.*

By the time the sun set the following day, I was on my knees swallowing him whole. It was simple, really, and while we didn't get sushi that first night, meeting for dinner at the other luxury mall, Phipps Plaza, across the street when he got off work became my nightly ritual.

He and I dated on and off for a few years. I remember lamenting to my cousin Tasha about how season one of *My Life with Freddie* was so much more passionate and sensual than season two—or three for that matter. Tasha being older, wiser, and gayer, rolled her eyes.

Well, we all know what season four will bring.

Loving Freddie was easy. He had amazing style, which he used to fill his own grown-up apartment with lux touches of flair. We adored each other in ways that were more intimate than mere physical touch. In truth, I think we needed each other to survive in Atlanta, because we weren't just faggots—we were genderqueer weirdos who played dress-up in vintage fur stoles and pranced around sticky dive bars in my dad's hand-me-down crocodile loafers. Freddie taught me about more than just fashion, he taught me about style. The more femme I presented, the hotter he thought I looked, which validated me in ways he couldn't've known at the time. Maybe he saw the girl in me. Maybe he was just attracted to the look. Either way, I loved it.

Our transition from lovers to friends was unspoken and organic. Few relationships of mine have been this way, without the need to specify what we are to each other or could no longer be. Being fearful of conflict or, frankly, honest conversations about feelings, made this evolution of our relationship feel even sweeter. I was grateful that Freddie didn't need to explain himself and expected the same in return.

And when I inevitably told him I was transitioning, I recall him sighing. *Finally, yes, good.* Then he hugged me and offered a classic, *I'm so proud of you, T.*

CRAIGSLIST

an unedited Journal Entry From 2011

I *think* my soulmate is whichever guy I'm dating—different guys, different times, but actually it's not. My soulmate is craigslist: the fantasies I create through craigslist because of the boys that I meet. Those fantasies are what truly give me butterflies, those false hopes of a picturesque, picture-perfect future that truly meets *my* needs.

I imagine the perfect apartment my boyfriend, Joe, and I will move into a year from now when my lease is up. (This is totally logical seeing as we met last week, and I'm eighteen so I'm grown.) It has granite countertops. A dishwasher. Washer AND dryer, none of that combo bullshit. Elevator with doors that open up into a quaint, third-floor West Village living room. The perfect puppy—let's say a Klee Kai, which is a kind of miniature husky—that's up for adoption. We'll name it Karl for Karl Lagerfeld. The husky used to belong to Mary-Kate (Olsen), but she wasn't responsible enough for it, so I took it off her hands (via craigslist, of course). The mountain house in Burlington for when we need to escape the concrete jungle; not that my—I'm sorry, *our*—perfect apartment isn't suitable. But Joe and I aren't your typical gays. We like the outdoors, too. Just not hunting, because that's cruel.

This is a wonderful way to while away the time. You may look up from your computer to realize that many hours have gone by, and you're on page 325 of potentially picture-perfect listings, and the coffee shop is closing, and your computer is about to die, and the charger is at your real apartment, probably getting used by one of your real roommates, who isn't named Joe, and it's cold outside, and you've procrastinated all of the real work you have to do all night to try and flesh out this…dream. The dream that your soulmate is on craigslist.

But you can't find happiness on craigslist. Maybe a comfortable couch, maybe a dick to make you happy for an hour, maybe some piece-of-shit DIY art project made by another unhappy person that says "happiness" on it…but you won't find the real thing. At least, I doubt you will.

Good luck, though…good luck, Tommy.

A LETTER TO MY EX-BOYFRIEND

In unpacking *The Lovers* I found myself searching ex-boyfriend's names on my computer in pursuit of historical clarity, hoping to find new pieces to fill in the blanks of my dysfunctional and endless puzzle. In my drafts of a now-defunct Gmail account, I found a letter I wrote to my high-school ex-boyfriend, Simon. We dated on and off for two years, bridging high school to college, and it ended because he wanted me to, frankly, grow up and get my shit together, but I wasn't ready yet. Reading this now, however, I see that I wanted something similar for myself and knowing that just a year later I would in fact get sober makes me grateful for Simon's wise-beyond-his-years ability to spot a train wreck and protect himself because it left me in an isolated state of having to dance with my shadow side, the devil within.

2012

Dear Simon,
How are you? I miss hearing from you, and genuinely miss our friendship and connection. I really want to know how

YOU are, not just "good," "doing well," "fine, thanks." But...how you are doing, feeling, what inspires you. I neglected all of those things the last months of our roller coaster of a relationship. But, I am writing to tell you now that I want to listen to you. Really be there with you and for you.

I cannot stop giggling right now. Thinking about how we used to be. Just reread an email from you titled "Things for Tommy and Me" with links to articles about feeling romantically stuck, love danger signs, and relationship advice. All fine attempts to fix our problems, but none focused on the clear issues at hand because neither of us really knows what those are. If only couples therapy was the norm, we'd lived in the same city, and my commitment level to both you and health were as high as they are right now. Maybe then the problems would have been solved and the choices made would have differed.

The other thing that I noticed the most going through our old emails is how much you really did care...you were so inexhaustible and willing to do whatever it took and put up with my shit for so long. And seeing that is making me realize that you will probably never take me back. But, what do you do when you are still so in love with someone and you don't know how they feel? Do you wait for them to talk to you...what if that never happens? Do you slowly try talking to them again? Or do you just lay it all out there, the naked truth, knowing very well that failure might be the outcome, but at least you tried your hardest, but still believing that the impossible is possible and he will say I love you too and let's do this thing.

I have loved you since the day I first saw you. An electric feeling—I can still feel it when I think about that day now almost two years later. Boom da boom, chills shoot through my body, and my heart rate doubles. I fucking want to know everything about this person and I want to know what they don't know they don't know and grow with them and love with them. Live with them. Move out of New York, get a cabin in Burlington, and have a family with him. With you. Or if you want to move to Paris, San Francisco, LA, Boston, Idaho, North Dakota, Texas, Mexico, Shanghai, Australia I'll go there, too. It doesn't matter where anymore or even when, just you. You and me. You and I, conquer what we want together, and grow as artists, people, activists, and inspire each other.

I just got out of a very insightful yoga class. We ended class with a quote that explains how we, as humans, are only able to truly hurt someone we love and often the people we do the most damage to are the ones we love the most. Odd way to start this letter, I'm aware, but with further unfolding it may make more sense.

I'm not going to assume where you are with this, but I do understand that you have most likely moved on since you are committed, as far as I know, to another person whom I'm sure is wonderful. But, through therapy (and yoga) I have learned that a good part of moving forward is making amends.

With that being said, it has become exponentially clear to me that so much of our struggles, mistakes, and my poor decisions about our relationship were made under the influence. I spend days and nights wishing to turn back time, but knowing that realistically it is not an option. If it were, I would have never left you on Skype during Hurricane Irene when I was in Keene. I would not have allowed such a ridiculous excuse as "independence to use drugs and drink" separate us back in May before arriving in Costa Rica. Furthermore, I would have thought before saying unforgivable things, kissing somebody else, or laying a single finger on you with harmful intentions. But I think the most important thing I have learned over the past few weeks is the sheer importance of honesty and integrity. It sickens me to think of how I used to treat and trick you and the amount of lies I would spin before getting myself stuck in my own web. How stupid of me to think that lying would make something better, and every day I am reminded of how lies are often what ruin friendships, families, and relationships. So I hope you will give me a chance to be honest.

You are it. The gravity that grounds me. You made me realize why people write love songs, and there is not one that comes on that does not remind me of you. I keep hearing about the importance of love and how, no matter what, if it's meant to be it will be. I'm not trying to force this…force us, but I need to fight for you because I love you and I know you love me, too. I want to be there for your successes, freak-outs, moments of doubt, and grow with you independently but simultaneously and in sync. I want you back. No, it's not going to be the same as it was before. No, I can't assure you that there won't be problems of some sort that arise. But… I can say for sure that I've had a long time to think about this and think about you without even really being in contact with you and I know that, whether it's now or ten years from now, I want a second chance. Well, I guess at this point it's more like a fifth or sixth chance, but who is really counting? I am willing to start slow. I am willing to just listen. I am willing to give you as much space as you need…but I do not want to live any more of my life without you being a part of it.

Please do not feel the need to respond, just know that I care for you deeply. I cannot even express how happy it makes me feel to know that you are happy.

You have told me I am your best friend, I will always be your best friend, and you will always love and care for me deeply. I want you to know that I still feel that way about you and I honestly know now that yes, I can live without you, but I would be a much happier person if you were back in my life. I'm childishly optimistic about our future. Still thinking that maybe we will be like Ross and Rachel.

It has taken a miracle amount of strength to keep me from jumping on a bus, plane, or train to DC and confessing my love for you in the middle of the street with roses in hand and unrealistic expectations fluttering in my heart.

Last semester when I wanted to get back together and you said not to force it, I respected that and said okay. So I tried to get over you, and partied, and did school and theater and went to Moscow and every day I thought of you and every day I tried to force myself to be happy without you and then I got back from Moscow and I stopped the drugs and I put down the bottle and I got back into therapy and I came to the realization that I'm not forcing this by coming here today. I'm putting my cards out on the table for you and expressing how I feel, but love isn't a one-way road and I'm not here to force you into anything or pressure you but simply to tell you how I feel about you. And I love you. I fucking love you. I haven't stopped thinking about you and I have a feeling that you haven't stopped thinking about me.

MY PISCES-AQUARIUS CUSP

After Simon and I broke up, I was dead set on being single. If I spent significant time with anybody, it was purely transactional. Like in the summer of 2012, between my sophomore and junior years at Fordham, I met a sweet man boy named Jackson who had central AC. Thank fuck. I feigned intimacy with him beyond physical contact just so that I could spend time in his Midtown highrise. I tried to help raise his French bulldog as a gesture of care. I don't think it worked. It only took a few weeks of me barely putting out—but drinking all his booze when he went to work—for him to gingerly escort me out of his home, never to speak again.

Then there was another J-named man. He wasn't particularly tall, but had a convertible. We'd wake and bake in his apartment on 10th Street, then drive around the city in a daze. That fall, Hurricane Sandy hit, and we left the city to go to my parents' house in New Hampshire. I eased into the role of suburban housewife pretty fast, making shitty stir-fry for my short-king. We'd get wine drunk and have sloppy sex on the couch before passing out to reruns of *Friends*. It was tender, and I liked him, despite him giving me my first STI—which we promptly treated at the Keene, New Hampshire, Planned Parenthood, but I didn't love him. So when we got back to the city, and he threw that word out, I broke it off. It was a first for me after being dumped so many times, but I was shocked by how naturally it came to me.

I can't give you whatever you're looking for right now, I'm sorry.

In mid-December, my friend at the time, Seth Lawrence, who was the only famous person I knew (he did a show about having a big dick in high school on MTV) was throwing a rager. We were fuck buddies who trauma bonded over our love of snorting Molly and watching the sun rise. That night, I railed two lines of a cocaine–Molly mixture in his bedroom on 12th Street, between 5th and 6th. It was 9:00 p.m., and I was scantily clad. Very quickly, I started to dance, feeling the drugs take over. The lights in the room twinkled like magic. I skipped out into the living room and took up a perch by the window, lighting a cigarette and talking to some random girls about how I was going to be an actor someday. *One day.*

Then I heard a piercing laugh come from the kitchen. Something about that laugh instantly spoke to me. It was familiar, like I'd known it my whole life. I looked over and saw a blond man, full of light and joy. He seemed like a J. Crew–clad angel. We locked eyes, and my stomach dropped. Without being conscious of what I was doing, I made my way over, grabbed a bottle of Jameson, and cornered him by the kitchen peninsula.

Take a shot with me.

He smiled.

I'm actually about to go promote tonight at YOTEL, but let me get your number. You're cute.

Oh, sure. Yeah.

It moved that quickly.

He took my phone and entered his number without ever breaking eye contact with me. So cool, so New York. The contact read Peter Zurkuhlen. As I stared at him, lost in his smile, my friend Cora approached and pulled on my jacket.

I hate to interrupt this, but Tommy. Our thing?

Oh, shit. That's right. Cora and I had a gig promoting at a club in Midtown, if you call the event space at YOTEL a nightclub.

Cora and I dashed outside and hailed a cab up to 42nd and 10th.

I'm going to marry that man, I said while giggling in the back seat, unaware of what I was manifesting.

I've heard you say that no less than twenty times this month, Cora dryly responded.

I texted incoherent emojis to Peter's phone all night, looked up the origins of his last name, and immediately started fantasizing about what our life together could look like. So much for staying single and doing hot girl shit all winter. I was smitten.

Ours was a whirlwind romance. It took less than a month before I'd moved most of my belongings into his tiny one-bedroom on Christopher Street. He would work his big boy real estate job at Brown Harris Stevens during the day, and I'd drink a case of beer while endlessly rearranging our furniture. It was a relationship of contrasts, at some turns blissful, at others baleful. Once, I sold a coffee table of his on craigslist without asking, and he screamed-cried for hours, explaining to me that I didn't understand what it was like to work hard for something. I cried, too, as I silently drank another case of beer.

I stole his independence in 2012. He should've been single too, newly out as gay and just moved back to the city from college in Kentucky. But we couldn't stop ourselves from falling into one another's arms. Neither of us was looking for anything in particular, but those early days were so heady, and I found myself committing to the bit, cosplaying domesticity, and this forced his hand. The weeks turned into months, which turned into years, and after my stint in rehab, we decided to get engaged. Which, if I'm being honest, is another thing I forced him to do.

★ ★ ★

By the time I was a few years into sobriety, I began feeling an insatiable need to prove that I was an adult who had their shit together. At twenty-one, I'd already gone through so much shit that I was ready to skip straight to my thirties. To me, that meant getting married, settling down, and adopting a dog. It was this compulsion that ultimately proved our undoing.

I was so wrapped up in trying to *prove* that I was grown, that I neglected to do, you know, the actual growing. Someone who was truly mature would have taken a good, hard look at our relationship and been honest with themselves about all the reasons we weren't right. Not that I was seeing something where there was nothing. What we had was a very real love, but it took both of us far too long to realize this love was the familial kind. We loved each other dearly, but we weren't *in* love. In hindsight, the signs were obvious. We never had sex, and before long, we opened up our marriage. (At the time, I thought this was yet another sign of our maturity.) Peter was safe. He was kind. On paper, he should have been everything I wanted. He fulfilled all the fantasies I'd ever had of feeling safe. He was always there waiting with open arms, the perfect golden retriever of a man. There was nothing *wrong* with our relationship.

There just also wasn't a whole lot *right.*

It didn't hurt that my parents loved him, and his parents loved me. Our families instantly bonded over their fondness for wine and other rich people shit. We'd gone to the same kind of high schools, had the same kind of friends, and shared the same idea of what professional success looked like; namely, independence and recognition. I got there a bit quicker than he did, booking *13 Reasons Why* when I'd only just graduated college.

Our dynamic was never quite the same after the show came out. He was happy for me, of that I'm sure. But I don't think seeing me achieve such a rapid high could help him from noticing all the ways he felt he still hadn't. He became despondent, fell into bouts of depression. It wasn't your typical sad-boy-depression, the kind that's easy to spot and glamorize. It was the kind that hid under a smile, the subtle depression that lingered and that only hinted at itself through things like biting down cuticles until they bled, or never saying anything more substantial than "I'm good" when asked how he's doing.

Once the show came out, my ego became an unstoppable force. My dark desire to get more famous, to make more money, to be inescapable, started trumping everything else in my life. I'd go away for weeks on end, only calling him when I needed help falling asleep. Otherwise, I was living an entirely separate life.

We were fucking other people consensually, and I began to resent him for not making more of himself. Not that I was offering much in the way of support other than my parent's generosity financially and some fun brand trips. I talked down to him in a way condescending twenty-four-year-olds do, made him feel like shit for not fulfilling his side of the bargain, not finding success "on his own terms," and ultimately tucked our marriage and home away on a shelf while I tended to my own selfish desires.

For a while, it worked. Or at least, it didn't fail. We moved to Los Angeles, bought a house, and began living lavishly. He started doing "glamorous" things like playing tennis with famous friends of mine. But it was fucking boring. Then, in rapid succession, the pandemic hit and I began to transition. Everything blew up.

It was a messy time. I started dating an actor in the summer of 2021, and left Peter back in LA to try and make sense of our failed marriage alone. We grew apart, dramatically so, our paths bending like the branches of a Joshua tree. Even after the actor and I split, too much had been said to take back.

I moved across the country again, and when I returned, he was there waiting for me physically but emotionally had already shut off.

THE NOMINEE
PART I

The decision to transition publicly was something I tried to avoid until I was backed far enough into a corner where I had to deal with it. I'd documented physical components of my transition on the internet but never spoke about the budding developments that might've been noticeable on my body. My style was shifting, sure. I'd cut all of my knee-length Thom Browne men's skirts to my midthigh and often paired them with skimpy tank tops, but I didn't change my pronouns in my bio or offer any *Days of Girlhood* stories to my followers. In truth, I was still navigating that sensitive time period of early transition and wasn't ready to disclose anything firm that I might regret later. For once in my life I was cautious and careful about my movements.

I found other outlets for my experience through art, like songwriting with Este Haim, which I never quite took to but the poetry of the medium helped me explore femininity and the inescapable grief of killing my boyhood to become the woman I am today. Friends of mine lent me dresses and offered me hand-me-downs and I started to call trans acquaintances who for a time became my sisters, offering me advice on everything from laser hair removal practices to tucking. When it came time to actually practice my tuck I took to YouTube and spent an hour trying to push my balls back into my body in bed with my friend Lena Dunham who was the best cis cheerleader a trans person could have.

She had already held space for a few trans people in her life growing up, like her brother, Cyrus, and knew the ins and outs of the medical institutions in Los Angeles, so when it was time for me to make my first HRT appointment, she helped me connect with the right team at Cedars to do so in private. Lena even went as far as attending that first appointment with me and jotting down notes in her little notebook with the regimen options that my doctor offered.

For a few weeks she was the only person who knew I was medically transitioning. I even kept it from my husband for a few months until I was brave enough to face the reality that, with him being a gay man, me turning into a woman would likely blow our marriage up as we knew it. Peter took the news as gracefully as he could and we tried to keep the spark alive as long as possible, but eventually the time came in 2021 to go our separate ways, albeit informally.

That spring Florence Welch, from the band Florence and the Machine, was staying in Brooklyn while she put the finishing touches on her album at Electric Lady Studios. One rainy day in April I crossed the bridge to meet her for a girly stroll and light shopping in her neighborhood. As we walked out of Books Are Magic it began to rain and our pace doubled. We were stomping in sync down the sidewalk, a cigarette dangling from my hand, when a voice yelled out from down the block *Tommy! Tommy!*

I thought it might be a crazy teenager who followed me on Instagram. While *13 Reasons Why* fame had simmered there were still some outliers who remained loyal to the show and its cast so it wasn't out of the ordinary to get stopped on the street for a selfie. But still, it shocked me, as I'd been fairly recluse in

Los Angeles going from my house to a friend's home via my own car. Also, a great benefit of walking down the street with a pop star like Florence is the freedom of being in their shadow.

I looked up, wiped raindrops from my eyelashes, and spotted a ginger-haired man walking directly at us. His hair was greasy and all over the place under a cap, his sweatpants stained, but he smiled like we were old pals and waved energetically as he approached. It was an actor I admired, someone I'd met years ago, but hadn't crossed paths with since the pandemic. It was The Nominee.

It's so good to see you—you look great, he said as he got closer.
Oh, thanks.

I introduced him to Florence and stood quietly as they talked briefly about music. He was preparing for a role in [redacted famous director] movie musical, which he's since dropped out of, and Florence graciously offered some wisdom and encouragement. His eyes were bright green and glistening and when he directed them at me my heart began to race.

Can I walk with you guys for a while? he asked, and we nodded.

The Nominee and I had met in 2019 after he saw a play I was in at The Signature. We'd occasionally run into each other in the city afterward. It wasn't anything special, he had a girlfriend and was straight, so I never thought much of it. But something about my transition shifted the way he looked at me. For the first time, I felt seen as a woman. He kept saying how pretty I was and I kept blushing. When we arrived at Florence's house she let herself in and I stood idly staring at my toes to hug him goodbye.

What are you doing later? he asked.
I have dinner with some friends…
Can I come?
Oh, that'd be great. Sure.

When The Nominee arrived at The Mercer Hotel lobby to join me and my friends for dinner it was, by and large, fairly awkward and uneventful. I wasn't sure what he was doing there, perhaps he was just lonely? But after about an hour The Nominee went to the bathroom and my friends told me that he was staring at me the whole time.

Like in a creepy way?

Like in a he likes you kind of way and maybe we should leave so you can…have some alone time together?

Oh, you don't need to do that.

Honestly, we're exhausted.

So they did. Once The Nominee came back to the table in their absence he sat closer to me.

Can I tell you something?

Sure.

I've been having recurring dreams about you.

Oh?

It's strange because we don't really know each other, but…a few years ago you I was telling you about an issue I had and you said so simply to not be hard on myself and I think about that often. And last night you were in my dream so when I saw you today it felt…it felt like fate.

Oh wow.

I didn't remember the moment in which I offered, likely unsolicited, advice to him in distress but it doesn't surprise me that I did. Often with strangers and friends I'd mutter some 12-step jargon or suggestion as a solution to temper their discomfort, and frankly my own. What is strange is as soon as he said he had a dream about me I remembered a dream I'd had about him a few weeks prior. It wasn't sexual in any way, but I had just watched his film with Michelle Pfeiffer and he showed up in my dream that evening.

I've dreamed about you, too.

Can I say something that might be forward, but I have to say it?

Yes.

I'm attracted to you. You are a beautiful woman.

The room started to spin at that moment, my heart audibly pounding at a rapid pace in my chest. Sweat began to collect

under my kneecaps and armpits and I was blushing in an over-
heated kind of way, a true flush. Never in my life had anybody
said those words to me so directly, especially since transitioning.
My body was coursing with desire for the first time in months
and I had to fight the urge to kiss him.

Well. Thank you. I'm attracted to you, too…

★ ★ ★

The next few weeks played out in a pretty standard love-bomb
cycle: he told me he loved me—I said it back; he disappeared and
said it was getting too intense—I cried on the phone with friends
about my heart breaking; he came to visit me in Mexico while
I was there for work—we talked about a future together; when
I went to visit him and his family in Montauk, he acted like I
didn't exist. My desperation for stability was so overwhelming
I would've killed someone if it made him more comfortable.
He became my boyfriend, even proposing to me in my car in
a parking lot. I declined, not even divorced yet. When he'd go
back to New York we'd talk on the phone for hours, multiple
times a day. When things got really bad he wanted me to go to
equine therapy with him over Zoom. His therapist was a legally
blind woman who never had a horse nearby as far as I could tell
but channeled horse energy. It was insane.

Yet one of the good things that came out of the relationship:
realizing afterward that I was not a straight girl but a gay girl.
Anytime The Nominee tried on a feminine character with me,
wearing my clothes, discussing gender expansiveness and cre-
ativity, I was more excited. Another good thing from the relationship: owning my transness publicly.

On a hot afternoon summer stroll in New York in 2021, we
were walking, hand in hand, across Bowery and I heard an un-
familiar *click click click* down the street. The sound came from a
camera in the hands of a short and stocky man.

Was that… I mumbled to The Nominee.

Yeah, I don't know. Maybe? he said.

While we had been spotted on DeuxMoi and stopped here

and there in our time together, this moment crystallized us as a couple in a public way that I wasn't prepared for. Within a few hours tabloid headlines circulated calling us friends and using he/him pronouns for me, even though I was out as non-binary at that point. I was terrified and furious. That photo ended up making some end-of-year listicle in print for the year's best (or maybe worst) outfits in *GQ*.

*I'm so sorry. I'm so sorry...*was all I could get out when I saw the photos on Twitter in the back seat of an Uber.

I think it's good. We look great and less work for us, The Nominee said.

Maybe he had a point. Maybe we didn't need to be so careful and calculated as we had been. I'm not sure we looked *great* but we looked at ease with one another and an Oscar nominee wearing his girlfriend's knee-high heeled boots and daisy dukes holding the hand of a newly blossomed trans woman confidently was pretty fucking cool. But deep inside I knew this wasn't the end. I was also fearful about what this would mean for his reputation, his career.

This moment ended up being larger than one photo and was very much the beginning of a new kind of celebrity and fame for me, one I've since strayed away from unless I'm actively promoting something. Playing a supporting role on *13 Reasons Why* in the era of Instagram meant I had control over my narrative and public perception. I could offer curations of my life and feign vulnerability to let people in while still remaining safely behind the screen. Unless I was hanging out with famous friends, I was allowed privacy by the media. That ended after the photo of me and The Nominee.

For the next few months anytime we stepped out publicly in New York or Los Angeles we were photographed. The more articles published the more angry I got. It was dumb; nobody knew I was transitioning at that point because I didn't think I owed it to anyone. When I shared my anger with The Nominee about the misgendering he suggested I just come out.

It'll be easier in the end...

I texted my publicist at the time, as well as my dear friend Sam Lansky, an editor at *TIME* magazine. Within a few hours there was a plan in motion, an editor was assigned, and the next week Torrey Peters agreed to do the interview. While we were friends at this point she had the utmost respect for journalism and set up some boundaries during the process to ensure a reputable piece got to print.

A few weeks later I arrived at a studio in Los Angeles to shoot the content, including a few fashionable looks, and a video companion piece wherein I shared the details of my transition and reintroduced myself as a woman. My team was with me: Chris Horan, who had been styling me for years; Kennedy who did my makeup at the time; Marty Harper who did my hair. It was joyous and filled with laughter and dancing. The Nominee was there as well and had Kennedy put a strong black eyeliner on him. It felt like we'd turned a new leaf at this point and perhaps our relationship could be nourished and prosper.

My reasoning for choosing *TIME* magazine to immortalize this moment was because it felt safe and irrefutable as a news source. They also had a pretty good track record of coming-out narratives—Josie Totah, Elliot Page, Ellen DeGeneres to name a few. It was the magazine that put Laverne Cox on the cover calling that time period the "Trans Tipping Point." I knew they would handle my story with grace. I figured this would be it: a quick little push in the press to adjust my honorifics and save me time coming out over and over again at work and with family and friends.

What I wasn't prepared for was how much attention this piece would garner. It quickly spread to CNN, *Vanity Fair, People Magazine,* the *Daily Mail,* and pretty much every outlet possible. Friends were sending me screenshots of Apple News Notifications about it and it was quite overwhelming and surreal. I'd told my extended family about my transition in an email just prior to the piece dropping, one that was simple and to the point and asked for no response, which was respected. I turned down every offer for radio and other press to talk about the *TIME* piece and learned how to navigate paparazzi who had another boost in photographing me and selling those images to gossip blogs and tabloids.

My star rose, but it felt very much like imposter syndrome since I hadn't done anything other than transition publicly to earn more acclaim. But it did lead to some fun work experiences and got me in the door to talk about things, like my filmmaking aspirations, and brought me closer to the queer community at large. Hearing that there are trans people who saw my article and it helped them feel safe, seen, and affirmed makes all of the other noise worth it.

The *TIME* shoot itself was so affirming, getting to see my femme body dressed properly with hair and makeup to support my gender (in arbitrary, very binaried ways I know) was life-changing. Having a majority of the public support at this moment in my life was and still is deeply meaningful and comforting for me. And the attention was fun. I am a rising Leo and chose to work in Hollywood after all. It marked the beginning of a whirlwind trans-girl tour, from fashion weeks to European modeling gigs to shooting jewelry and beauty campaigns, auditioning for girl roles, and getting my movie *I Wish You All the Best* green-lit.

The Nominee and I broke up in an ugly, unsalvageable way, but I was stronger because of it. I was free for a few months to say yes to any and every desire or opportunity that presented itself. I'd never been so carefree and liberated before and, since the dust has settled, and I've come out of trans puberty, I'm not sure I ever will again. It was one of the rare moments in my life where I can say I felt really fucking strong. I felt like I was in control of the lion, that I could mount it and ride off into an abundant future.

THE DJ

"Good boy. I mean girl—fuck—boy—girl. Yes, girl," he repeats between moans, apparently unable, in his marijuana haze, to decide exactly what I am. It's clear that he's trying to do the right thing, to make me feel seen, even though his dick is in my mouth and his body is already tingling with the anticipation of orgasm.

I just take it, because what else am I going to do? We're alone in a gaudy Airbnb in the Hollywood Hills, the musky scent of Hinoki Fantome hangs heavy in the air, and he literally just won a Grammy. In truth, I'm thankful for his penis being shoved up against my uvula, because it helps me stifle an awkward laugh at the way his accent ping-pongs all these pronouns around the room before my ears catch them.

She. He. Her. Him.

It's not his fault. I'm not fully realized yet. The notion of "womanhood" remains as of yet a myth for me, because to be a woman takes work and patience.

Oh, how I desperately try to perform for him. Let's call him Michael.

Donning a brown floral minidress and knee-high boots, I

feel good about what I'm serving; the "what" in question being double-A titties and a sizable ass from all those years of gym-rat-faggotry. Squats, bro, no homo. At home in Silver Lake, just a few miles away, I'd spent hours staring at myself in the smudgy bathroom mirror I share with my ex-husband, ready-ing myself to go on my first date with a man as a transsexual. Globs of mascara à la Twiggy and a flush of Dior blush swiped across my cheek. On second thought, was it giving Twiggy or Boy George? Probably a bit of both.

Whatever. Okay.

This is what I'm thinking as I look in the mirror:

You look cute. Well, maybe just fine. No, it's cute. And your legs give woman—strong woman—but woman no less. And you practiced walking, and you've been working on your voice. It'll be good. Great, even. And he knows you're fucking trans. He sees the journey, and he's cool with it.

He isn't even out as gay, even though it's clear based on the DM history that he would've been down in the "before time," and sure, I haven't come out yet, but isn't it obvious? And fuck coming out anyway.

Driving on the 101 makes me dizzy. Am I having a panic attack, or is it just the LA smog? The whole city sprawled out before me like a damning map of my psyche: stuck in the grit and grime of Hollywood, the mythical promise and allure of the beach looming far beyond the horizon. I must've shit four or five times before I finally left for his Airbnb, and yet, I still maybe have to shit again. Nerves, man. Moments like this re-mind me of the anxiety I felt before stepping onstage as a kid, nerves like laxatives.

Cigarette smoke billows out from between my lips and through the slight crack in the window, which I refuse to roll all the way down to save the small mop of hair on my head, and too much wind makes me cry anyway.

Usually a date at a house means fucking, but it's the pandemic, and in the pandemic it means being safe. So there's nothing to be nervous about. Someone on TikTok called her dick a chunky vulva, and the thought strikes me that with clothes likely staying on, there'll be no need to disclose my own chunky vulva.

"You look hot," he says, midbite of the Kismet Rotisserie chicken I brought for us to share. My body roars to life in an explosion of heat, because no one has said this to me, not this directly, since I started 'mones.

It feels at once good and uncomfortable. I've always had weird triggers around compliments, especially ones that turn on aesthetics or have a sexual flair, which probably stems from years of hating myself and my body and all the men in their early thirties who fucked me when I was a teenager when I didn't know better, didn't know about trauma or consent, just knew how to keep going so as not to feel a damn thing.

After a pause, I muster a quick "Thanks," and I take all of him in for the first time since I got there.

I'd spent the initial thirty minutes or so trapped in my head as I tried to understand who in their right fucking mind would decorate a house this way—neon and white and wood and clean with an insane view, and then just, like, random ugly-fake pop art sprinkled in, and some of the cliché taxidermy that never makes sense in Los Angeles.

Like most men in Hollywood, Michael is shorter than I expected, and awkward, like he should be a computer programmer, not a man who headlines stages around the world. Still, he's sexy in a smart, cool way—way cooler than I could ever pretend to be—wearing wide framed Alessandro-era Gucci glasses because he actually needs them to see, and not just for the academic pretense. Or blue light.

I find myself studying his thick glass, wondering how my image might be getting refracted through them. I had just mentioned that I was, ya know, trans, because it would've felt like that big elephant in the room, and my cross-dressing days were over. He's scratching an itch on his bicep, itself hidden under a white shirt that's draped over his lithe frame in such a way that I know it's expensive, like The Row or some shit, cascading down until it tucks into Hedi Slimane–cut jeans.

God, I wish I could turn my brain off right now and just breathe and be here and take a fucking compliment.

Instead, I start to pick up the dishes. It's my go-to. Also, I want him to watch me walk away. Years at theater school, and I only took one thing from it: distance creates tension—good, bad—and you can use it to your advantage. So I create some distance, feeling his heat radiate toward me, and the faggot inside me takes over.

There's no way we aren't fucking. I'm literally washing your plates and saving your leftovers, and you're just letting me do it. Taking in my body. Watching me play house like some '50s homemaker coursing with Valium. More than anything, I wish I could slip into a Valium haze right about now.

In a flash, we're on the leather mid-century couch, quiet and intense. His veiny fingers trace my leg—smooth—and his lips press against mine, and my clit might explode at any moment, tucked so tight between my legs. I can see the imprint of his dick through the tight jeans.

Then, we're in bed, and I turn around for him to undo my dress. He kisses my neck, my back—you know the song. Except, is there a pussy for him to kiss? My neck, my back, my tucked penis, and my crack just doesn't have the same ring to it, phonetics be damned. For a moment, this thought consumes me. But then before I know it, we're naked, and somehow, even with a seven-inch clit, I feel like a woman. Michael is in charge. His manhood defines my womanhood, and he moves to go inside me, but my body just won't relax enough to let it happen, so I flip around and throw my face between his legs. Plan B. He takes the generous offering, combs fingers through strands of my hair, and fucks my face rough in a way that feels familiar, comfortable, perfect.

Until he says, "Good boy."

The rug is pulled out from under me. When he says "boy," all I can feel is the stubble pushing out of my chin. Suddenly, it's a countdown to the end, I think. I have to get through this, to suffer, it's no longer a pleasure. Not because it isn't fun, or it doesn't feel good, and not because I think he's a bad person, but because I didn't sign up for gay sex. It's these sorts of moments that make me miss drinking and crushing any pill I can find to snort up my nose.

But then I hear a faint, "Sorry baby," and I realize he's trying, and I should try again, too. This is just one, one of many, and it could be way worse. He's a reputable person, we have mutual friends, it's good. We're good. And so I ride him until we both cum. An orgasm so intense that it's painful.

It's the first time that I'd really cum in weeks. Because of the pain. When you start transitioning, this thing happens that nobody tells you about, or at least nobody really told me, where your chunky vulva stops getting hard as regularly, as freely, and carelessly as it used to. Like, you just don't wake up with boners anymore. This means that when you do get hard, and hard enough to cum, it fucking hurts, because the skin is stretching itself out again after being dormant for so long. And then the actual semen shooting, or pouring out at this point (what's left of it)—liquid something—also hurts in a different way, like you're on your last rep at the gym and pushing through the pain.

The death throes of masculinity.

Your dick is trying so hard to produce anything at all—to fertilize the fucking air, because it's too stupid to know there's no child coming from this—that it will work overtime to get the job done. And I'm glad it does, because the feeling after is yummy and sweaty. That moment of putrid beauty in which skin sticks to skin. It feels so goddamn good when I fall into him, and in the quiet that this moment opens up, my brain does that dumb thing. You know the dumb thing.

Am I in love with this person? Am I going to be here in this bed for the next two weeks until he goes back to Iceland? Am I going to get Icelandic citizenship and are we going to have babies? Like, am I going to get that uterus transplant I read about that feels too *Brave New World*, and we're going to just, like, be this cute, straight-passing couple in Reykjavík, and I'll learn Icelandic and how to make Skyr, and we'll have teas with Björk, and we'll fuck like this until we die?

And then he sort of slides out from under me, and I come back to earth. To the bed. Embarrassment. "That was so good, baby," he says as he swiftly puts his clothes on, like he's embarrassed of his body now, too.

"Going somewhere?" I ask as I put my underwear on and scan the room for my dress, doing my little after-sex dance.

"Just meeting friends at a party thing I'm gonna play at…"

And I wait a few beats for an invitation, because he just came all over my fucking spine, and we're industry adjacent, and it's not like we'd walk in holding hands. But then…

Nothing. So I go to the bathroom. And I touch myself up and down. And I look at my five o'clock shadow. And I kiss myself in the mirror. And I get in the car. And I call my friend Ella. And I spill.

"Can you fucking believe—"

Just two girls talking about boys.

THE SUN

upright: positivity, fun, warmth, success, vitality

reversed: inner child, feeling down, overly optimistic

My eyes rest on the next card: The Sun.

Glorious.

Out on the water, the sun sparkles, and I can't look away. I grew up spending summers on a murky lake in Alabama—beautiful but dark and deep, you couldn't see below your belly button when you jumped in. But here the water is crystal clear all the way down to the beautifully rocky floor.

When we are out wake surfing, I should be paying attention to my friends, but I'm too enamored with the bubbly white crash of the boat's wake, and how it glistens in the sun above us. My breasts ache for the sun's warmth right now, budding from my masculine pecs, begging to be nourished. The sun here is unlike anywhere else I've ever been.

I have often opted for shade when given the chance, and prefer a crisp winter to a soggy summer. The sun is all too much for me to take in most of the time, blinding, forcing warmth upon me when I don't want it. It's always been a symbol for me, defining the concept of joy from the time I read my first picture books. Some of my worst days have been the sunniest, and some of the best cloud-covered and moody. But out here, in Montana, I beg the universe and the sun gods for more time to relish in her glory.

RISE

I think I've watched the sun rise more times than I've seen it set. Now that I'm in this strange stage of life where I've begun to truly enjoy the simple pleasure of a 9:30 p.m. bedtime, this is a fact that I'm proud of. I watch the world awaken, feel invigorated. But this wasn't always the case.

You've seen more sunrises than you have sunsets.

This thought used to sting me. It's true, I have, and for a long time it was because I couldn't sleep. The uppers weren't mixing with the downers, the Xanax I'd swallow trying to curb the twenty lines of coke I'd snorted on any given night wasn't working, and the voice in my head would get louder and louder, screaming—

You're fucked-up. You don't know how to sleep. You don't know how to exist in harmony with the movements of the earth and stars. You don't know shit. You're a fucking drug addict, you don't know how to not use. You don't know how to love yourself. I hope you die in your sleep. You don't know anything…you don't know…you don't know…you don't know.

I'd pass by mothers with strollers, runners, the city waking up, people doing adult people things with their time here on earth, productive things, and think I can't watch another sunrise like this. I have to stop wasting my life. But I didn't know how. All I could do was stay beholden to the morning bedtime ritual I'd cultivated for myself, like punishing myself for whatever crimes I'd committed in the night. I was, for a time, living on 14th Street and 8th Avenue in an overfull, illegal three-bed above a brothel that I shared with two other gay men. One was from Australia. He was the tallest and had the smallest room, which was just half the living room converted into a makeshift bed area. No windows or closet. The other was an otter from New Jersey, and we used to drink together from time to time. I think they both regretted inviting me into the apartment as soon as I'd moved my stuff in. Perhaps it had something to do with the months I slept with a mattress on the floor and nothing unpacked because I couldn't get around to doing it, what with the drinking and all.

When the hour for sleep arrived around 9:00 a.m., whether alone or with a boy, I'd pull the cracked vinyl shades down over my window, shrouding the room in darkness and transforming it into a Stygian twink cave. The type of place you'd expect to find Edward Cullen getting bottomed. What sparse beams of light made it through the blinds illuminated the permanent cloud of cigarette smoke that hung heavy in the air. A diary written in Parliament Lights.

I'd roll over onto my side, stare at my nightstand, perpetually covered in a blanket of dust and cocaine residue. Resting atop it was a cityscape of empty cans of whatever shitty beer we'd picked up at the bodega downstairs. Or swiped from a bar and stuffed into the pockets of our trench coats, the condensation seeping into the fabric and creating strange little Rorschachs that the rest of the world could only interpret in one way: those bitches are addicts. But still, I needed sleep. I needed my heart to stop pounding through my fucking chest. And I'd just tell myself, quietly, usually in a fetal position, *It's okay if you die, just get some sleep. It's okay if you don't wake up, just go to sleep...*

Stealing those beers always reminded me of this woman Laura

that I partied with in Atlanta from the ages of, like, fifteen to nineteen. She looked like a New Jersey housewife that got elected Queen of the Fags on a bachelorette weekend in Atlanta and was never allowed to leave again. Brown, thick hair framed her chiseled face, a skeleton of a body swaddled in oversized rag & bone T-shirts and Helmut Lang leather leggings. Always in a blazer, with a love bracelet and the loudest, raspiest laugh you'd ever heard. She must've been in her mid to late forties. We met through her best friend, Billy, who supplied our drugs. His lot in life is still unknown to me. He wouldn't even let us inside his apartment when we'd go to pick him up. He, too, was a shell of a man—short and skinny, high-pitched voice, always ready to read you for filth.

Laura would fill the base of her Hermès Birkin with Long Island iced teas from Blake's, a glorified trailer on the edge of Piedmont Park that was my—and every other faggot in a two-hour driving range's—safe haven. We'd pile into Billy's Audi A3 and ride over to whatever warehouse afters or shithole drug den we'd been called to and finish them off.

I sometimes wonder what else she kept in that bag. It was her prized possession, a celebratory classic 35 she rewarded herself with when she hit five million dollars in sales at Jeffrey, this wet dream of a luxury women's wear boutique in Phipps Plaza with a more famous outpost in the Meatpacking District. Or so her story went. (Both locations closed in 2020.) I used to go there as a kid with my mom's American Express and pick out all her clothes for the season: work trips, weddings, bar and bat mitzvahs, New Year's Eve parties...

But back to sunrises. Or, actually, one sunrise in particular:

The morning of May 13th, 2013. My eyes are glossed over, squinty as the sun rises up and presents herself to all of creation. It's my twenty-first birthday, and I keep thinking how underwhelming and meaningless the occasion feels given that I've spent the last decade blacking out.

I'm with Peter, my boyfriend, in a taxi driving across the Williamsburg Bridge. I peer through the window, looking out at the East River. My phone is dead, my toes and fists are clenched. Peter brushes his fingers through my hair, getting stuck in my blond locks—matted and greasy, but still soft. At least, he thinks so.

The night wasn't supposed to end this way. I should have been at LaGuardia an hour ago to catch a flight to Burlington for my old prom date Jessica's graduation at UVM. But I wasn't. And now I'm here, suffering from a mild form of delirium tremens in the arms of my lover, while Jessica's probably applying the finishing touches to the winged eyeliner she always pulls off so well. My throat is raw from cocaine drip and cigarette smoke.

Numb, tired, ashamed.

I keep stretching out my chapped lips to feel their sting.

Why do you do it?

Peter's voice. Gentle, a little gravelly. He's looking down at me, his face suggesting no emotion in particular. I stare back at him.

What?

He slowly exhales.

Like, I'd get it—I mean, I get why people do drugs. And obviously you do you, but you just seem...

His voice trails off, and he looks out the window, perhaps in search of an answer to his own question.

I follow his gaze, then keep going, up toward the sun and her white-hot light, and I hope she'll blind me. If I'm lucky.

You just don't seem happy.

I reflexively wince, and suddenly I'm swimming in a Technicolor sea of blue and purple and orange, sun dots seared into my eyes, and for a moment I wonder if I'll get my wish. And then without opening my eyes, without thinking, really, I say—

Because I don't really know what else to do.

A few months prior, Peter had been waiting for me at 89 Christopher Street. A different sunrise. I'd spent the witching hours of that morning dragging the limp, overdosed body of a friend of a friend down the hallway of her building after hours of speedballing together. She was svelte, but every muscle in her body had gone limp, so I had to lug her down the hallway, past apartments belonging to all manner of blue bloods. By the time we got into the elevator, her blond hair was crazy with static from the carpet.

I remember thinking, *How the fuck did this happen?* Like, forty-five minutes prior, the three of us were laughing our asses off, and then Mitt, the boy, and I got lost in a conversation about nothing in particular, until we realized she'd been silent for a while. I walked over to her and her skin was a sort of gray-blue and freezing cold. Fuck fuck fuck fuck fuck.

Mitt urged me not to call an ambulance, fearing he'd be blamed if she was actually dead, but my stubbornness—or really common fucking sense—prevailed, and I did it anyway. It came in a blinking blur of red and blue, and since the girl and I bore a resemblance, the paramedics didn't question how we knew each other, or whether or not we were related, or why the fuck I was dragging her out of this expensive apartment building. They just scooped us up, and having no shame about my drug game, I told them everything that she'd consumed to the best of my knowledge.

Nothing is more sobering than riding bitch in the back of an ambulance. White lighting, cold metal, too many colors clashing, sirens significantly less loud on the inside, everybody's radios going off, and the sterile smell of antiseptic. When the girl came to after a few blocks and some Narcan, she refused to look at me—clearly any chance of us ever being friends was gone. Not that it mattered much. When we pulled up to the hospital, I left without saying goodbye. I was running late, as per usual, and Peter and I had a flight to catch to Cancún for spring break.

At Peter's apartment, I fell into his arms, just as I did whenever we'd watch the sunrise together, and broke down. I couldn't tell him what had happened or why I was late, just that I'd been "out." He'd already done the packing, so we quietly rode to the airport holding hands. My phone vibrated. A text from the girl. Just two words:

fuck you

Relatable.

On the flight, I wrote monologues about how this trip to Mexico would heal me (lol)—how I would come back to the city a new man, no more hard drugs, just the occasional "responsible drink."

When we got to the resort, something Azul, I couldn't even get drunk from the watered-down, all-inclusive booze bottles in the hotel room, so I gave up and detoxed in the scorching sun.

Back in the city, it went on like this—tiring, depressing, strange, numb—for a few weeks. In February, I was arrested for drug possession in the Lower East Side after two undercover cops found me doing key-bumps outside a shitty club, and it was late March or early April when she overdosed. I was starting to see other people in the extended circle of druggies and theater kids and people I called "my friends" disappear, drop out, dissolve into…something or nothing. Ashes to ashes. At my normal dive bar haunts—the type of places where promoters with names like "Jagger" would practice dark arts on young, unsuspecting twinks—bodies were moving around like musical chairs. It was a heady time.

I recently stumbled across a little diary entry I wrote around that time and felt like throwing up:

It's a great feeling to realize that I now get drunk off a glass of wine…a sign of maturity, and also an example of the truth about drinking: it's a sport, and if you don't practice often, you become rusty.

For me, this is a positive:

1. No longer will I be spending the unnecessary dollars on a half-pint of georgi's to get me to the point where I can tolerate strangers and other members at a college party.
2. All I need is my sippy cup half filled with some cheap pino to turn my Sunday into a funday.
3. My hangovers are not nearly as severe and my want for cocaine is pretty much nonexistent.

It's clear to me from this and other entries that I was in fact *aware* of my addiction and trying to sort it out. A myth I'd tell myself early on in my recovery was that I couldn't understand how I got to the place of checking myself into a rehab at twenty-one, but looking back at it now, ten years on, I can see baby T was slowly putting the pieces together all along.

But this moment of nascent awareness didn't last long. It only took a few weeks before I was digging back into my old Rolodex of dealers and scoring my usual everything-but-the-kitchen-sink cocktail of pills and powders and flowers and mushrooms and vials and whatever else the vagrant in front of me was hawking. Some cocaine to bring me up, Xanax to help me sleep, Molly to sprinkle into beverages and blunts, and, of course, my newest addition (who was rapidly becoming a series regular): heroin. I would get it in white powder form to snort, because shooting up just wasn't for me. And so, to nobody's surprise, really, but my own, by the time my birthday came around, I had multiple eight balls at the ready and a night of mediocre Brooklyn debauchery planned. It was to include some dumpster fire gay bars (that definitely did not go on to survive the pandemic), and the wild mix of friends I somehow managed to hang on to during my rock-bottom moments.

It's just—I'd understand if you were enjoying yourself, but you seem…

We're back to 2013. Peter again. I want him to stop talking, my ears are bleeding and my brain is struggling to keep up. Like, shut the fuck up.

I don't want to be presumptuous, it's just—and I'm not judging you, I promise. I'm just curious, like, why do cocaine and whatever else if it makes you so...

Miserable? I manage to croak out.

Yeah.

I don't know... I don't want to do it, but I can't...not.

I struggle to remember the end of this conversation, because really the only thing that matters now is that it happened at all. That for once in my fucking life I could honestly say to someone I didn't know why I couldn't stop doing drugs. That I could not sneak, lie, cheat my way out of confrontation, like I did when I said I was going to rehab a few summers prior to avoid getting expelled from Semester at Sea for sneaking drugs onto the boat. Peter opened a door for me to finally admit for once that I didn't want to do drugs anymore and that I didn't know how to stop. A seed planted, and the sunrise fertilizing it.

★ ★ ★

A few weeks later, a banging on my front door jolts me awake. I'd been kicked out of my 14th street apartment and recently moved into a spare bedroom on Washington Street with an elderly gay couple who spent most of their time in Rhode Island. I look out the window. I look out the window, bleary-eyed and foggy-brained, to find the sky beginning to brighten. June 6th, 2013.

Martin Thomas—open this door now—

Fuck. Is that my dad? Really sounds like my fucking dad. I run and open the door, revealing a breathless, terrified man who I hadn't seen in months staring at me. Angry and sad and exhausted. He pulls me into a bear hug.

What are you doing here? I asked him, still half asleep.

We're going to rehab. You called me.

Oh, that. Shit. He's here, it's today. And he's right, I did call him, I guess just yesterday or maybe the day before. It's all blurry.

I thought you were dead... he says. Crying.

I laugh.

The AC was on high, and I guess we just—

I called you, I called Freddie—

You called Freddie?

I always call him when I'm worried that…

Well. I'm here.

Are you packed?

Pretty much. Sit down, I'm just going to grab my shit.

Peter is awake in bed when I come back in. He stares at me blankly, then offers a tender smile. Also, I'm not packed, but who needs anything at rehab anyway?

Are you sure you won't come with us and drop me off? I ask him.

It's your thing. I have to work. But you know I'm proud of you. Really brave.

Okay…but you're not going to break up with me, right?

No. I'm not going to break up with you, he says. I don't trust him.

I nod—*Okay*—and start to collect the assorted clothes and books and God knows what else—all the things that currently constitute "my life." Why? To bring to rehab, where I'm getting a small discount because my cousin has been there twice in the past twelve months. I'd always idolized her, so maybe it makes sense that her getting sober would turn on some lights for me. Like this is all just me trying to act cool for the big kids.

We're driving out to East Hampton. Being in a confined space with my father means endless tapping of my toes in anticipation of whatever serious-but-not-too-serious, slightly-misguided-imparting-of-wisdom-cum-jeremiad he has cooked up. Except it never comes. I look down at my hands, marveling at how their square shape mirrors his own, only a little smaller. Larry Ivan Dorfman, born in the mid-fifties in Brooklyn, Jewish with a signature crew cut and an infectious smile. A teddy bear of a man. His hand is gripping the gear shift and I'm thinking, *Oh, shit. This time is different. This time he's quiet and reserved.* When

I'd called him and told him I wanted to try to get clean, he'd simply exhaled, and in the same breath, said, *Finally. Thank you.*

He assured me he'd be on the next flight out of Hartsfield-Jackson, but I asked him for one last night alone with Peter. He obliged.

Here's something dark: When searching for a rehab that night, I literally Googled "celebrity rehab fancy." I wasn't famous, not even close; I was just delusional and unwilling to go somewhere that would ask me to mop floors or give me cafeteria duty. Because heaven forbid this shit actually be, you know, *hard.*

The closer we get to East Hampton, the more I regret my decision. A pit in my stomach starts growing, screaming at me to jump out of the car *Lady Bird*–style (even though *Lady Bird* was still a few years off—bless you, Greta).

I don't think I can do this, Dad.

You can.

I don't know. Maybe I jumped the gun.

You didn't. But if you did, you'll find out soon enough. We're here now anyway.

I press my forehead as hard as I can into the cold window of the car—except it feels more like a hearse.

Fuck.

ROAM

A few days into my first sleepless week at The Dunes, I started to redevelop a relationship with the sun.

It was summer, and I'd pace across the wet grass as beams of heat broke through the early morning fog, or sit on the balcony I shared with Frances, my rehab neighbor, both of us chain-smoking because we couldn't fall asleep, and he'd regale me with tales of women he fucked as we watched darkness give way to dawn. Each night felt like the longest of our lives.

Frances's voice was high-pitched, a trait you would expect from a twink, so I couldn't help but be amused when he squealed about pussy this and pussy that. It was his forty-third year around the sun and his fifth time institutionalized for a heroin "dependency" as he put it. Multiple overdoses in one lifetime, and he was still struggling. I was probably the youngest in the whole place by at least five years, and most of my rehab peers had been in and out of treatment centers, chronically relapsing and draining their bank accounts just to give sobriety another go.

Like Patti, who slept in a bunk room with a woman named Apple. She was a twice-divorced schoolteacher in her late sixties who proclaimed that she'd rather spend all her money on rehab and be buried in a plywood coffin as long as she could be buried sober. This felt a little trite to me. Like, do we really give a fuck about sobriety if we're already six feet under? But whatever she needed to tell herself. All power to her.

Standing in the communal kitchen, which had a skylight that allowed the sun in, I'd fixate on her shadow, with its shaking hands and frail legs and booze-bloated liver belly, which reminded me of the shadows of the women in my own family who suffered from the same ailments. I knew I didn't want to be like her. Or Frances. Or Apple. Or anybody else there for that matter. I also didn't think, at this early point, I had a problem that rivaled theirs. I was a young party boy, that was all. This was par for the course. I wasn't a lifer. Really, what this all boiled down to was my own arrogance, *I'm better than them.*

Nonetheless, I did begin thinking a lot about the idea of a higher power, or the universe, even a God. Not that I had much of a choice—a key tenet of AA is that you have to accept a higher power—but I was surprised to find myself taking it at least somewhat seriously. Steven, who the program aptly nicknamed Spiritual Steve, worked with us individually as we got to the second step: *We came to be aware that a Power greater than ourselves could restore us to sanity.* He was tall, boney like a fawn, balding with a shaved head, wearing baggy work wear and John Lennon glasses.

He challenged me to list coincidences in my life that were too good to be true. Did ending up in the same jail cell as a kid I knew from middle school count? At one point, when Spiritual Steve pressed me for an answer on how my relationship with God was going a few weeks in—because if I didn't find one soon, I'd probably drink and drug myself to death—I looked up at the sun and exhaled: *She'll do for now.*

★ ★ ★

Believing that some great, almighty thing got me sober was impossible. I mean, didn't *I* make this choice? I took agency, I was in control. I got here, to this McMansion on Long Island that the rehab purchased from a gay couple during the recession in '08. The estate, while beautiful, made a lot more sense within that context. Every room seemed to be designed to fuck or party in and, while nothing felt particularly homey about it, I was happy to be in the confines of these walls, afraid of what I might do to myself if I ventured out. We all shared this sentiment, this relief of having nothing to do. That is, after the initial panic of realizing that this was going to be life for many, many weeks ran its course. Privatized rehabs are rich adult summer camps disguised as institutions, complete with tennis courts, equine therapy, a heated pool and sauna, massages and yoga treatments, 6:00 a.m. acupuncture (which I opted out of because our practitioner openly shared his early onset Parkinson's with us, and a few wrong pokes in my ear was enough for me). We even had a private chef, this ridiculously hot guy from Costa Rica who rode around in a convertible Porsche he was gifted from a housewife he had an affair with. Moreover, there was an unsettling sense of levity: movie nights, meetings where we'd all try to one-up each other with just how crazy our pasts (and presents) had been, pints of ice cream every night, trying to get high by hoarding melatonin gummies that were offered to us in the evenings, etcetera. A wide range of the adults were stuck at the age when they had started drinking—balding, wrinkled, brain-fried teenagers. One man, who made his money in waste management and came here from New Jersey, had a collapsed nose. They were just running around like idiots and doodling in the margins of their worksheets. I could've stayed forever in this safe haven; we all could've. Except Charlie, a seventeen-year-old uber-rich prep school kid, who ran away three times back to his parents' beachfront house in Sagaponack. Eventually they gave up on trying to find him, and I suspect his parents gave up on trying to fix him. I hope he's still alive today.

I wasn't particularly concerned with staying 12-step sober, as my plan was to kick the drugs and learn the tools needed to drink responsibly, like an adult. In truth, my primary concern was Peter, and what the fuck he might be up to in the city without me, and why he couldn't respond to every single text message or support me in the ways that I felt I needed to be supported. This is how it felt, anyway. I hyperfixated on him, digitally stalked him, gaslit him to no end. I unconsciously manipulated every part of our conversations in an attempt to wrest some semblance of power back into my life. He was my proverbial punching bag and I would incessantly challenge the clear boundaries he was trying to set in order to seek his love, attention, and validation.

Fucking cringe, right? So if your attachment style is to strangle your partner until their eyes pop out of their skull, you're not alone. It baffles me, when I think about our life together—the nine years we spent as each other's person, all the bad shit I put him through—that he stayed. But that's his nature: dependable, able to remain optimistic through the worst of the worst, straightforward, caring. All of which was antithetical to my nature at the time: run on fumes, waves of pessimism fueling manipulative tendencies, scheme and be a baby and get my way no matter what. His skill remained refraining from the temptation to follow me when I cried wolf. I needed to be loved, I just didn't know how to ask for it respectfully at twenty-one and newly sober. And now, in my thirties, as I look back on that time, I really do see a sad girl scared of being abandoned, with an inability to trust the man who so clearly loves her and she's in love with—or clinging onto for dear life—and she'll do anything to sound-act-seem-speak like a grown-up. And so she spins out, stuck in an anxiety-k-hole, and harasses her boyfriend she met months prior to checking into rehab over text and voicemail and hanging up mid-sentence on the phone when she's not getting the response she wants.

It's easy to look back at conversations like this, ones where the evidence is so blatantly clear, and see when I'm gaslighting or manipulating. To recognize it at the moment, however, is nearly impossible for me. But, like anyone, I desired attention and needed to be loved.

The day I got out of rehab, Peter was away at a family wedding, and I felt like I had something to prove. I knew staying sober in rehab was easy, like duh, but I feared coming back to New York—on a Saturday no less—could be a disaster. There was never going to be a good time to reassimilate into the bare bones of the life I'd left, though. *Just get through tonight, you can do anything for an hour,* I said to myself, forehead pressed against the glass window in the back seat of a black Escalade, fingering a pamphlet filled with the times and locations of meetings around the city and shaking from forty-five-minutes of nicotine withdrawal.

As the city came into focus, so did my inner panic. Arriving at my sublet apartment in the Village, the same one my dad had dragged me out of a mere five weeks earlier, my body went into a manic hyperspeed. I paced the apartment. The gays (read: my two roommates) were out in Provincetown, and when I opened the fridge to grab the Brita, I came face-to-face with an open bottle of rosé. This was the worst-case scenario. I mean, it was *right there.* No one is watching. Almost like the universe was intentionally dangling a bundle in front of my face. But then, as I stared at the bottle, the strangest thing happened—I became calm. Not in a, *I'm at peace* kind of way, but more, *I know what I have to do now.* I poured it out in the sink, rubbed my palms against the bristles of my newly buzzed head, leaned back against the closed fridge, and started crying. I didn't want to be alone, but I didn't know what my options were, and I was set on proving to myself that I was capable of readjusting to the world by staying sober and not calling Peter to talk me off a ledge.

He was my rock. And that's why I loved him so much. He babied me appropriately, he tied me to the bed and fucked me consensually, and when it was time for me to step out of the nest, he encouraged me to jump, even if it meant falling hard on my face. His faith kept me going through that first year of sobriety and for that, I will always thank him; I will always love him; I will always cherish his patience. Being with him placed all of my selfishness and egotistical behaviors under a microscope, carving out new spaces for me to burrow in and learn more about who exactly Tommy was. It was precisely the recipe I needed for success at that time.

But it was a recipe that was going to take a long time to prepare.

RIPEN

Eventually, as the hours turned into days, and the days into weeks, and the weeks began to multiply, sobriety started to feel like the best fucking thing that ever happened to me. Turns out, I *did* take AA—and myself—seriously. The world had never been more lush, food had never tasted so good, and my passion for sun salutations inspired me to enroll in yoga teacher training while I figured out what exactly my life plan was going to look like. Because of course I had to figure it all out that first year of sobriety.

The summer sun would fill me with an urgent optimism as I Citi Biked my way from a 7:00 a.m. meeting in Greenwich Village, out to SoHo for yoga, then back to the apartment I moved into with Peter at 89 Christopher Street, then eventually acting classes in Tribeca. I would experience the highest of highs, teetering on the edge of mania at times. Turns out the sober girlies had a term for it: *pink cloud*. It's the euphoria that freshly sober addicts experience early on in their recovery. They feel like they can do anything. But it doesn't last forever.

While my head was caught in the pink clouds, I started making new friends, other young people who also thought their life was over when they gave up parTying—emphasis on the T for Tina—and traded $17 vodka sodas for $17 cold-pressed juices. And in spite of my aversion to the religion of it all, I did talk to the universe, in my own sort of way, thanking her for watching over me. I connected with my ancestors, dove into therapy, did my step work. I told everybody I was sober now.

Aren't you proud of me? Aren't I amazing?

Most people my age thought it was a phase, an unnecessary or even annoying one, but it was my way of holding myself accountable to the world. As the child of a salesman, attraction was my agenda. I sold the world around me on AA and abstinence and the whole *Ohmmmmmm* thing. I was flying with Helios, mindful of Icarus, and avoidant of all things Hades in my life.

The first three years of my training at Fordham for acting felt far, far away, like they belonged to the old model of myself. Model, like, 2.7, whose system had crashed in early June of 2013 from a combination of poorly cut cocaine and cheap bourbon. And that shutdown represented a big data loss. Certain files became irretrievable. I lost parts of myself. Being sober both incentivized me to be as successful as possible, and terrified me because I didn't know who I was without alcohol and drugs.

Sometimes, though, you just have to throw shit at the wall and see what sticks. This was a time of extensive reinvention. The first and most obvious thing to really integrate into my identity was acting. I'd been acting or dancing or performing since I was, like, four, but this felt like something new. I was no longer an addict trying to act; I was simply an actor now. To make it all feel real, I made a website for myself, Tommy Dorfman— the *ACTOR!!!*

For over a decade, rampant drug abuse had fried my brain, bankrupt me of most of the neurological prerequisites for sustained joy. A few months into sobriety, suddenly my neurotransmitters began to come out of their comas, and began bubbling to the surface. Dopamine! Serotonin! Oxytocin! Endorphins! *Was the world always this beautiful and harmonious?!?*

First it was the taste of ice cream, like had anything ever tasted as good as Ben & Jerry's classic Cookie Dough? I cried halfway through a pint. Wiped out from step work and yoga teacher training and being on my fitness, not to mention the mental Olympics of early sobriety, I sat down and opened a pint from the deli—as I'd been doing all summer—and it tasted like a fucking Bollywood film dance number was going off on my tongue. Euphoric. A small, simple life thing suddenly opened a portal of feelings and emotions I didn't know existed. Sobriety became the best fucking thing that had ever happened to me and I wanted everybody to follow suit.

I preached to friends, drug addicts, family members, strangers; pushed through glossed-over eyes to try and make the world see how much happiness sobriety fostered. In hindsight, it was less about convincing other people to get sober as much as convincing the world that *I* had my shit together. That *I* was growing up and on the right track. And it worked. That first year, I felt every fucking feeling possible, basked in the glory of my own humanity. My own fragility. And yes, my own sanctimony. I cozied up to the voices in my head over a cup of fresh ginger-mint tea, and I tamed them. I laughed from my toes. I screamed-sang as I skipped down the halls of the LGBTQ+ Center on 13th Street, choosing—*claiming*—happiness as my default.

And just as quickly as I'd ridden my sobriety to the top—so too was the crash a complete fucking whirlwind. Soon enough, I was thrown back into the reality and melancholy of it all. Church basements and Waverly Diner lost their luster after the first ten or so visits, and I began to wonder about the other parts of my life that had been ignored. Like, what the fuck would I do if I had to actually live for the next sixty years? I still had to be a real person? Wasn't focusing on my sobriety enough? Wouldn't everything else, like, take care of itself?

So while this lust for clean, healthy living and working a strict recovery program laid the bedrock for my life today, it only temporarily fed the beast, the hunger for success that resided deep within me. I wish I could say that being sober and becoming a yoga teacher or healer or real estate agent or whatever the fuck would be enough for me. I needed to find an outlet, though, a reason to live far beyond the emotional labor of Getting Well.

That first year, I started working in retail, hopeful that it would turn my fashionphile curiosities into a full-fledged career as CEO of Balenciaga or Comme des Garçons someday. But I lost momentum. The stale, corporate world of hocking luxury goods proved…stale and corporate. Running up and down seven flights of stairs with a handful of Alaïa shoes at Dover Street Market was perhaps not the creative rush I needed. At least not to feel successful. Team sports weren't really my thing either. It felt like there was a whole bunch of wasted potential. I mean, getting sober meant I could become anything, didn't it?

I knew I wanted to go back to acting at some point. It felt like there was an inevitability to my return to school. It had been a lingering thought in the back of my head ever since getting back from The Dunes. In truth, it would keep me up at night. When was I going to deal with this? When was I going to re-build the bridge I'd burnt? There was a part of me that simply didn't want to. I carried so much shame, felt at once guilty and embarrassed about how the whole thing had unfolded, and it would have been far easier to hide behind the good parts of my sobriety and pretend the hard parts simply didn't exist and never would. In the end, though, I had too much pride and gusto, coupled with a healthy fear of disappointing my family, not to return to Fordham and the fluorescent basement which housed their drama program, and to prove to them I was worthy of their acceptance.

After having dinner with an old advisor of mine at a Mid-town sushi spot, they let me return, and I did some version of the above, accumulating more credits in my final few months of school than I had my whole sophomore year. All said and done, I managed to graduate in 2015.

When I think about The Sun card, a radiant and abundant

energy/inner power—a strength that isn't ego driven, but stems from something greater, more profound—comes to mind. I rode that newfound sense of purpose and expansiveness, but it hasn't been a steady progression. At times, I've lost the sun. Either the moon presents herself, or, more likely, complete and utter chaos is wrought by my own hand, and selfishness wins over. But even in the moments where darkness prevails, it's a connection to the sun, and all her life force, power, prosperity, and balance, that I tap into to lead me toward her light.

Finishing school was a chore but the months that followed were some of the most liberating and important moments in my life. I was free to work part- or full-time, so I got a job at a Baz Bagels—a lesbian-owned bagel shop on the Lower East Side— thanks to my friend Lisa, who I'd grown up dancing with at Atlanta Ballet. I woke up at 5:00 a.m. to open the shop most mornings, watching the sunrise on the J train from Chauncey to Canal, reading novels, memorizing scenes for acting class, taking silly little Instagram photos in the Nashville filter.

The restaurant was bright pink—a shrine to Dolly Parton and the Golden Girls—and we had free reign of the Spotify so I'd dance around blasting Destiny's Child at 6:00 a.m. and pine over the cute skater boys who lined up in droves to nurse hangovers with everything bagels, iced coffee, and schmeer. I'd flirt and give my regulars coffee on the house. We also had a lot of celebrity clients who filled the tables during weekend brunches. It was sweet.

Around that time my best friend and roommate, Quinn, got an audition for a show called *13 Reasons Why*. He was one of the lucky graduates who scored agents from our Senior Showcase. We worked on the sides together, helping him prepare, and I asked him to send me the script and who was casting. Later that night I took to the internet and found that I'd taken a workshop with one of the casting associates.

At the time, I'd managed to get a manager—albeit a man in his late twenties that worked out of his cellar apartment who was dating a friend of mine that worked in membership advising at Equinox. Michael was his name and we tag teamed to get me an appointment for the show. Luckily they were doing a wide search for a variety of roles and their open-call process secured me an opportunity to audition for Clay, the lead, at first and see if there were other roles that might be better suited for after.

As for the *13 Reasons Why* callback process, it was grueling. I wasn't sure what it was supposed to be like in the first place. At my first audition, for the role of Clay Jennings, I was giving my best teen-heartthrob-male-drag. I tried to channel a brooding Robert Pattinson, wearing less fitted jeans and a simple army green T-shirt that my friends said brought out my eyes. It was January, I believe, so I layered the T-shirt with my Canada Goose. My reading was sufficient in proving I could act decently, but obviously I wasn't right for the role.

A few weeks later, I had a callback for Ryan Shaver, described in the breakdown services as a "tweedy poet." He wasn't explicitly gay in the character description but I figured since I was being asked to come back he had some sparkle. For this, I wore a gray high-water wool Thom Browne suit, shirt, and tie that I procured from working at Odin—a menswear store—on Lafayette that sold the brand. It was 2016 and the brand hadn't crossed over to the mainstream yet.

When I walked in, clearly nervous, the casting associate simply said *This is a good thing, Tommy. So just try to breathe and remember that they want to see you for a different role because they all really liked your first audition.* I took a deep breath, felt my feet on the ground beneath me, and started on Ryan. The associate worked with me on the scene a few times until he was pleased and sent me back onto 8th Avenue.

Weeks turned to months of waiting after that first callback. I slung bagels and OJ at Baz, chewing up my cheeks in anticipation. *No news is good news*, my friend Lisa said to me one brunch shift. *Sure…* I responded, lacking any assuredness whatsoever. But finally, just as the flowers were starting to bloom on my block of Decatur Street, I got another callback. This time I would be reading for Ryan, again, but with director Tom Mc-Carthy (fresh off an Oscar win for *Spotlight*), Diana Son (who wrote a play called *Satellites* that my school had done on their main stage a few years back), casting, and Brian Yorkey (whose musical *Next to Normal* changed my life forever). How the FUCK was I going to pull this off?

The audition was at 3:00 p.m. in Midtown so I decided to go from work to the gym, shower and change there, and then hit an AA meeting in Greenwich Village to buy me some time. A few fellow sober alcoholics from the rooms walked with me up Broadway to Flatiron where we sat chain-smoking until my appointment. I wore the exact same outfit, down to the underwear, because I was both superstitious and hopeful that they would recognize me immediately. I blacked out during the audition. I couldn't believe I was standing in front of ten people, baring my soul in this way—I just had to steady myself in the script and the world and try to ignore their presence. We flew through the scenes and at one point Tom McCarthy laughed, which took me by surprise because I didn't think the scenes were all that funny. But I suppose my innate seriousness and earnest approach to the material actually lent itself to the comedy of the moment. When I finished the scene I asked if I did something wrong and he chuckled again, *No, no, it was perfect—I just hadn't seen it done like that before. Thank you for coming in.*

Certain I'd blown it, I tried to push the entire process out of my brain and make room for potential new opportunities. Though no other auditions for major shows came, I found myself doing some fun readings downtown and a twenty-four-hour play festival, which Jeremy O. Harris's early work was a part of, at Theater for a New Audience in the East Village. My only rule was that I wouldn't work for free, but a $25 stipend and a MetroCard was enough for me. Once I workshopped a play where the director asked us to improvise jacking off...that was fucking weird. Otherwise my minimal experience in the downtown off-off-off-off-Broadway theater world was pleasant enough to pass the time.

The thing was, I fucking loved acting—and still do. It offered me a way to express emotions, feelings, insights I harbored in my day-to-day life. It's still the only time I feel totally, irrevocably in the present moment. I revere actors as a director now and in my twenties, as I was crafting my own style of acting, spent all my free time binge-watching Cate Blanchett movies, making sure to see her anytime she performed on stage in New York. Her production of *The Maids* from their Lincoln Center stint is seared into my psyche. I admired Tilda Swinton, Fiona Shaw, Sidney Poitier, Julianne Moore, and Viola Davis the most at that time. Any chance I got to see theater, I saw it, even when it meant sneaking in (second acting) because tickets were too expensive.

Actors doing amazing work were my little shimmering suns when I was coming up in New York. Anna Deavere Smith was my Jesus Christ, Alan Cumming my Mary of Magdalene. John Cameron Mitchell was God. When I wasn't watching movies and TV shows and going to the theater, I was rereading classics, like Shakespeare, and more modern writers, like Tennessee Williams. I read *A Little Life* in three days, unable to escape the painful world Hanya Yanagihara generated. My therapist had recommended it to me and I now know that bought him at least another six months of sessions and processing with me. I read on the subway, on lunch breaks at work, sitting alone at cafes between acting classes and AA meetings. Patti Smith's *Just Kids* was gifted to me from my dad and I devoured it at Waverly Diner. It changed my entire outlook on artistry and creation at the time, on relationships and all kinds of love and grief. I got deep into the catalogs of James Baldwin and Joan Didion, and spent a weekend reveling in Sally Mann's *Hold Still.*

THE HANGED MAN

upright: pause, surrender, letting go,
new perspectives

reversed: delays, resistance, stalling, indecision

I pull the next card: The Hanged Man and can't help but laugh at the tarot's humor in this. My heart aches because I look just like the man in the card: blond hair falling down in a triangle shape, a blue jester's uniform, red tights, and yellow ballet flats that I could never find in my actual size if I wanted to. He hangs from a branch with his right foot, his left leg bent in a pirouette sort of shape. But the sun illuminates him. There's hope there.

The Hanged Man means waiting: waiting for your moment, waiting for the dust to settle, waiting for the storm to pass. Or, in my case, waiting for your breasts to grow and skin to soften, waiting for the estrogen to work its magic from the inside out and move the fat around your body to be more feminine—whatever that even means. Hormone Replacement Therapy comes with no guarantees. There aren't any road markers, no clear signs of when it's "worked."

I look out at the lake and wonder how long I will have to wait. They say it takes three years on hormones before you see the full power of their physical effects. That feels like an eternity. Some cards depict

The Hanged Man as a chrysalis waiting to hatch, and that resonates more with my idea of change. Or maybe it's just that this image is less gendered. I don't know. On the outside, I am still very masculine. My muscles are toned to perfection and I spent yesterday on a boat, completely shirtless, wearing board shorts. I'm reminded to purchase some women's bathing suits to try when I get home.

HELL

You're wasting time and it's only going to get harder if you don't do it now, Hari says over a Marlboro Gold in her perfectly pointed manner.

Okay. But I'm not... I mean, what about Peter?

Hari shrugs, like it is what it is.

*We're literally MARRIED—like—*I take a drag, my eyes drift into the kitchen where he is typing away on his computer—*like I want to be with him.*

Do you, though?

She asks this with a devilish smile on her face. I hate that she's right, but I can't do this again. I can't handle another major failure. Being a drug addict felt like enough "fucking up" for a lifetime.

Peter fixed things. Everything. People trust me now, like my parents. They see me as a grown-up. Marriage is what adults do, okay!? But he's a gay man. Do I really want to be married to my gay best friend after I transition?

It's more complicated than that. It's him. It's work...

Work isn't going to fulfill you forever.

That's rich coming from one of the most driven artists I know.

But it's still my livelihood. And what if I'm not sure? I just need more time...

What about when you're eighty?

Huh?

Like, for me, I imagined myself old and I just knew I couldn't be an old man.

Her question stuns me. Aging has never really felt like a possibility. Even at twenty-five, I already feel like I'm living on borrowed time. I light another cigarette as I try to envision being old. I see white-blond curls, trousers, a blouse. I see my grandmother.

Fuck.

If you start now, you'll stunt some of the residual brow bone growth that's coming for you, she says, taking another drag.

Moving from hypothetical speculation to actual logistics makes this all feel so much more real, and I realize that she's completely right, and I begin to cry. My body freezes. My breath shortens. My toes go numb.

I recognize it immediately as a panic attack. My anxiety has been on a slow incline ever since moving to LA three years earlier. Having a trans roommate certainly didn't help. In truth, I'm jealous—I just haven't recognized it yet. Jealous that she has it all figured out, jealous that she's a year younger than me, jealous that she's so beautiful. I could never be, like, a *pretty* girl, could I? But there's also a quiet disdain, because I know that she sees me, even though I'm not ready to be seen. I can't hide the girl inside while being clocked morning, noon, and night. And now that we're having this conversation, a whole new element is thrown into the mix: Could these new panic attacks be a product of gender dysphoria?

In an effort to shut my friend Hari up, I manically outline a half-formed plan: I'll make a fuckton of money exploiting my six-pack and playing the gay best friend until my mid-thirties.

Then I can take a break, disappear to Spain, get all the work done, and reappear as the fully realized version of myself. I mean, I've made it a quarter century. I can handle another decade.

Right?

She laughs as if to say, *whatever, girl.* Then she casually strides downstairs into the basement studio where she lives.

Left alone, I touch my body. I start with the muscles, their smooth contours. Then I press deeper, into the hard bits, bones and all. Then I retreat, lightly fingering my chest hair, suddenly in disbelief that it belongs to me. I put my hand in my sweatpants and feel my dick.

What is that? I mean, what is that really?

My body is suddenly a prison. It feels like it is built in an image that my mind does not agree with. I take out my phone, quickly Google *how to transition*—but before anything pops up, I shut it off. This is too much to take in, to strategize, to rationalize. How is this so? How am I just now acknowledging something that, if I'm honest with myself, I've always known to be true?

I go back to my pipe dream plan. The one with Spain and abs and such. It's got a fatal flaw: it doesn't solve the problem of the here and now. What I am supposed to do right this second? In a span of five minutes, I've not only finally admitted to myself that I might be hiding a fundamental truth about myself from the world, but also that I need to step away from the man who has given me everything.

I know that if I don't make the jump, he won't ever leave me. He's too good that way. We'll just continue coasting, our non-monogamy drifting us further and further apart from each other. Not a nightmare, sure, but also not the fantasy one imagines when walking down the aisle. I see a vision of my future that I don't like. And that scares the shit out of me.

But that fear elicits an even stronger swell of courage, and in a moment of total clarity, I make a pact with myself.

I'm going to transition, but I'm going to do it on my own time. It doesn't need to be in a decade, it can be sooner, but it also doesn't need to start today. There's some comfort in that, knowing the end doesn't have to be as painful as the present moment. That I have agency over my growth.

But the feeling of relief is fleeting. Just as quickly as it came, it is replaced by a crippling realism. I understand now that by giving my future self license to transition, I'm locking my current self in gender purgatory. It's a bargain I have to make, because for now, the alternative—blowing up my life by transitioning— is too overwhelming.

One step at a time. One fucking step.

I take one last drag of my cigarette, then I turn to look out the window. It's early evening in LA, and the sun is beginning to sink below the trees. Just outside the window, thick stalks of bamboo glisten in the waning light. They look an awful lot like bars, I think.

TIME (2020)

Time moves differently now. Days move like months, weeks move like years, and months, well…

Actually, I don't know if that's what I mean. It's more like there's a whole month's worth of life jam-packed into one day now. The way my body changes, the way I'm processing things; it's like I'm going through puberty at warp speed. Making up for lost time.

And still…three more years they say. In just six months, my flesh has begun to expand and contort in ways that I did not imagine possible. My nipples are swollen in this beautiful, supple, jiggly way. I had dinner last night with friends at Chateau Marmont and one said—what did she call them? *Perfect little boobies, little fashion boobies! I used to have those, before I had kids.* That was nice. I told her she could feel them, and she did, and my body was aroused, which I immediately suppressed because there's no way I'm transitioning into a fucking lesbian—haven't I been through enough? Being trans isn't enough? I'm not even a woman yet, so—

What does it mean to be a woman? Am I a woman when I

stop growing facial hair? I've seen cis women with facial hair. They're in the *Guinness Book of World Records*, in encyclopedias, in memes, on TikTok, in my family. They're real. They exist. So, it's not about facial hair, then. What does it mean to be cis? Or trans? What does it mean to be a woman? And piggybacking off that, how do I become a woman? As I ponder this, I realize it's a question I've been asking myself since childhood. Shit.

What did you want to be when you grew up?

(This is the world asking me this question.)

Well, I—I wanted to be a girl, but not just any girl. I wanted to be a princess. I wanted to be royal. I wanted you to give me a hug, pick me up, twirl me around, dress me in taffeta. I wanted you to see me—Princess T— I wanted—want—you to…see me and celebrate me. I wanted you to help me grow.

And so, the answer is: I don't know what it means to be a woman, much less a girl, or whatever…whatever even counts these days. I shave my face every single morning and every other afternoon if I have plans. I shave my face, and it bumps, and it hurts, and it stings. I shave my face and spend thousands on lasers that aren't doing what they're supposed to do quickly enough.

I shave my face.

And every time I shave my face I wonder: What does it mean to be female?

DREAM GIRL

i found you
drifting through my dreams last night
    taking over me inside

old skin decomposes
bury him in roses
changing names and poses

hair shades of blue
nails pointed up to the night sky

no one can save me
i wasn't prepared to find
you in here waiting but—

you found me
sleeping through days and night

pills chasing
never water only wine

dead eyes started closing
you came in and
took away the poison

now she's living
breathing in that new daylight
basking in that new daylight
she came to save me now
she came to save

RAGE

The sun, as most are well aware, is a star—a searing hot ball of plasma with an incredibly dense core. It burns so bright that you can hardly look at it without going blind.

It's no wonder that early tabloids found this a fitting metaphor to describe the burgeoning phenomenon of modern celebrity, a new class of people who were trying so hard to be seen it almost hurt your eyes.

There was a period after *13 Reasons Why* came out when I found myself getting recognized with an alarming frequency. It happened almost immediately. Hardly nine hours after the show made its midnight debut on Netflix, Alisha Boe, my co-star, and I walked down from her Silver Lake apartment and got in line at Sqirl, what once was a hipster fueled cafe with decent food that fell apart after their jams were found to be mold-ridden. We were in line, the sun blasting on our sunglasses faces, when all of a sudden we heard a little squeal. We turned around to find a trio of girls behind us, backlit by windows, we couldn't see them well. But then our eyes adjusted, and I realized who it was: the fucking Haim sisters. They walked up to us gabbing about how they'd just binged the show, how much they loved it, and we took photos together. We exchanged numbers, and I marveled at this—was it always this easy? Was this how famous people interacted, just casually exchanging personal details outside of overpriced cafes in LA? Was I even famous?

A few days later, back in Brooklyn, I was riding the A train uptown, reading *The Goldfinch*, when dozens of teenagers started to fill in the gaps between me and other travelers. There were lots of whispers—*Is that him...?*—and finally a short, stout brunette teacher asked, *Are you that kid from that show that deals with the girl with the problems?* To which I said, *I think?* And phones flew out, arms wrapped around my body, a queer kid cried. Seeing me was apparently so overwhelming that it helped him come out. They were a whole class on a school trip from Florida. While certainly exciting in some way, I found the experience overall to be harrowing. I was sweating, embarrassed, scared. At the next stop, I quickly said goodbye, then bolted out of the train and up the stairs at West 4th, where I hailed a cab back to Bed Stuy. The whole ride home, I replayed the incident over and over again in my head. It consumed me, and not in a good way. It was my first swarm. All because of a few hours of television.

When I got home, I locked myself in my apartment for a few days. Sure, I'd dreamed of a moment like that for my whole life. Only now that it'd come, I was utterly terrified, fucking ashamed even, because I didn't feel deserving, like my work hadn't qualified me for that level of attention. And, on that train, it felt like a violation, as if the comforting cloak of anonymity had been stripped off my back and thrown to the ground.

It's perhaps no wonder that I was unable to set down roots in Los Angeles. A city of angels, of stars, of the sun, of all things astral.

I could never pierce that smoggy veil and find the beauty that so many of my friends spoke of.

I lived in LA from the winter of 2017 to the spring of 2021, in a trendy, hipster neighborhood called Franklin Hills, stuck between Los Feliz and Silver Lake. The bedroom of our bungalow was a dark oceanic blur of blue wallpaper, and waking up in it every morning, I found myself beset with a sort of dull depression, which was only made worse by the perennial sunshine. It was like the sun was teasing me, provoking me, daring me to unpack why I wasn't happier—with the sun, with the city, with Peter, with my own body.

I did a play in 2019, *DADDY* by Jeremy O. Harris, in which one of the characters said the line, *"if it's summer every day, when even is it?"* And it haunted me until my return to New York.

Betty Gilpin summed up life in LA nicely in her 2018 op-ed for *The Hollywood Reporter*:

> Being an actor feels like your ego is on a violent pendulum swing between a field of cashmere and a casual tub of knives. Depending on how the industry is treating you that hour, you either feel like a Mariah Carey sultan or a near dead irrelevant possum, flashing people for change on the 405. Spend too long on either side, and you're a terrible lunch partner.

Maybe this is why so many celebrities love drugs.

As someone with no prior connections to the business, I never quite learned how to make myself feel like I was "on the inside." Even as I got to be very close with amazing people, I couldn't help but do more observing than participating, at least behind closed doors. Out in the world, though, the public viewed me as just as much a part of the fame machine as all of my way more famous friends. Imposter syndrome, ever heard of her? I was a supporting actor in a very successful, but ultimately not earth-shattering TV show, while the people I was hanging out with could literally alter the culture with a three-word tweet. That's a startling amount of power I wasn't even sure I wanted nor could contend with.

I've heard it said that the later in life you become famous, the more normal you are; I think this is generally true. But I also have close friends who have grown up in the public eye and are some of the best human beings I've ever met, while I've hung out with actors hot off their big break that are fucking *foul*.

By 2019, I was starting to feel as if I was losing any semblance of groundedness I might have ever had. Most of all, my sobriety was starting to take on the shape of a fun house mirror in the sense that, even though I wasn't drinking or using, I still found myself being "altered" by the headiness of Hollywood. In many ways, it felt like I was experiencing the disorienting fallout of drugs—the lack of perspective, the depression, the disillusionment—without actually, you know, drugs. That was when I realized I needed to get out. My sobriety was too precious to risk for anything, much less something that I fundamentally disagreed with.

So I came home to New York. It was the summer of 2021. Peter and I had finally agreed that a divorce was likely the best way forward. We'd been separated for quite some time, living more as best friends/roommates, but the jig was now up. He decided to stay on the West Coast, I decided to go back East. It wasn't a permanent move, more of a "let's post up here for who knows how long and see what happens." Almost immediately, I wound up dating an actor who still lived with his director dad and stir-crazy Juilliard-trained mom in Brooklyn. Things were going fast, and we even talked of moving in together, fantasizing about elevator-into-apartment lofts in Nolita and weekends escaping to Montauk. While those things didn't happen, thank GOD, apart from one nightmare weekend with him out East, the seed was planted. I decided—regardless of how this relationship panned out—that in order to move forward in my life, I needed to move back to New York. LA was done.

★ ★ ★

The first time I lived in Los Angeles was for a summer camp at the New York Film Academy intensive, sandwiched between my freshman and sophomore years of high school. It was—and perhaps remains—a breeding ground for nepo-babies and aspiring actors and filmmakers with parents wealthy enough to pay for six weeks spent living in Hollywood. I made some very close friends that summer. We'd spend our evenings railing Adderall and listening to Ben Kweller, while our days were filled with running around Universal Studios, making silly short films, and smoking multiple packs of Marlboro Lights, courtesy of my friend L.T.'s mom, Susie.

L.T. was from Austin, Texas, and I fell in love with him on the first day of camp. His unruly blond hair and Ksubi skinny jeans, paired effortlessly with layered spike belts and remnants of last night's eyeliner, gave him a Pete Wentz edge. And he fell in love with me. It was platonic but deeply connected, and I'd never met a straight boy so comfortable with my queerness.

My memories of how the camp was organized are hazy, likely dulled by years of doing copious amounts of drugs, but I distinctly remember seeing L.T. for the first time on the second or third day we were there. He was emerging from one of those brown trailers you see at suburban schools under construction, standing under an oak tree, confidently sucking down the last drag of a cigarette. His presence was grounded and fearless, remarkably self-assured for a fifteen-year-old. I was flamboyant and newly out, my life modeled after characters from *Queer as Folk*, which I had recently downloaded from iTunes and watched religiously. It was my gay Bible.

But his self-assuredness was unmatched. He drew me in like a magnet. Shyly, I asked to bum a cigarette, having smoked through my pack I brought from Atlanta, and feeling itchy from nicotine withdrawal. Without a shade of judgment, he laughed and handed me a cig. It was a moment straight out of a movie, right there on a fucking studio backlot. We instantly clicked, and were inseparable for the rest of the summer.

Once I met L.T., I saw an exit cresting the horizon, and knew I had to take it alone.

★ ★ ★

Within the first day of having met him, I maneuvered to align all my classes with his. As a second-year student, he knew how to rig the system in our favor, having already learned the tough lessons, like how to sneak out and not get caught, where the counselors stayed, and their patrol habits. He was also at the center of a strong core group of friends from the previous year. Among them were Sosie Bacon—the on-and-off-again girlfriend of L.T. and daughter of Kevin Bacon and Kyra Sedgwick—and Meltem, a Turkish heiress dripping in Cartier love bracelets and Miu Miu bags, whom I idolized.

But I was young and naive. This was the first time I'd met people from other countries. Meltem had an effortless coolness that seemed rooted in her extreme financial security, and perhaps, the fact that she was older than all of us at seventeen.

In spite of all this financial privilege, it was an open friend group. Chain-smoking was pretty much the only barrier to entry. Did you smoke, or did you not? Did you drink, or did you not? What about hard drugs? Weed didn't count. I guess you could say we were the bad kids at camp, migrating in and out of classes, lunch breaks, and excursions like a family of ducks, L.T. being the mother duckling, us the chicks that followed along.

By the end of the first week, we'd firmed up connections for alcohol, used Meltem's Amex to book a black car that took us to Chinatown, where we procured our first fake IDs, and collected enough Adderall to get us through the rest of the summer. We blasted Fall Out Boy and Tom Petty songs in our apartments, rearranged the furniture, and stayed up all night laughing until we cried. I rarely ever strayed from the pack that summer, and if I did, it always involved a boy.

Like one time, a Swedish transplant named Nathaniel and I found ourselves hooking up in a living room. I don't remember whose. He had stumbled into the apartment during one of our "parties," which were really just small gatherings of people we trusted enough not to snitch. Nathaniel and I were sloppy drunk in a bedroom closet, and when I went down on him, I was surprised both by the size of his dick—it was massive—and that he was uncircumcised. I didn't know what to do with all the extra skin, so I ran out and, like the asshole I was, gossiped with my friends about it.

Then there was Phillip, the son of the drummer of a famous rock band in the 80s. He was managing some C-list actors who lived at Oakwood, the apartment complex that we were housed in for camp. One day, he walked up to us as we were lounging by the pool to invite us to Teddy's, a now-defunct nightclub that hosted the elite it girls of the time. (I'm fairly certain this is where Paris Hilton infamously called Lindsey Lohan a fire crotch.) For the rest of camp, Teddy's was my safe space—when I could get there. I could pick up a bottle of vodka to guzzle and nobody blinked an eye. Mama, I made it!

Phillip was twenty-five, and incidentally, a chronic heroin relapser who ended up taking advantage of my teenage body on multiple evenings when I was too obliterated to stave off his advances. After that summer, it would be years until I saw him again. I was deep in my own addiction and for a few foggy weeks in 2012 we hid out in the Jane Hotel where he was living, emptying the mini-bar, bumping heroin, and smoking joints the room service boys delivered with our meals.

In spite of the fact that I had this extravagant summer camp experience in LA, the city itself never stuck. Sure, the people were fascinating—watching tabloids come to life gave me a sense that the world was in fact larger and more complicated than I could've imagined growing up in Georgia. But it was also clear to me that Los Angeles only prioritized famous people; everyone else was treated like shit. I vowed to not go back until I had a real reason to be there. Like, you know, a job. I needed to be able to earn my own way into clubs like Teddy's without relying on the help of pedophiles. Besides, my heart was already set on Broadway and New York City. I wanted to be a *real* artist, a *real* actor, and the hunger for fame that seemed to permeate the City of Angels wasn't alluring to me.

What I loved most about Los Angeles were my friends, and our little ragtag rich kid revue would be just as in love with each other no matter where we were. The lesson I took away from that summer was that life is a whole lot more fun when you're living it with people you like—even if there are major cracks looking just beneath the surface.

★ ★ ★

I returned to Atlanta depressed and depleted. I was heartbroken, having fallen so deeply in love with my camp friends, and the glitz and glamor of those six weeks. If nothing else, Los Angeles had provided me with an image of what was possible. I began my sophomore year of high school with one mission and one mission only: I was gonna make it the fuck out of Atlanta. (This is kind of ironic to me now, given that it's essentially overtaken LA as a Hollywood production hub.) The first step was being the star of our school's musical theater program. I'd done ballet since as long as I could remember, but I decided it was time to hang up my pointe shoes. My bones were aching from it, and now it was going to prove too much of a distraction if I was going to land a supporting role in that year's production of *West Side Story*.

The camaraderie I felt doing *Urinetown* freshman year of high school was parlayed into summer camp, and by the time sophomore auditions rolled around I was determined to get any role just to be in the company of my fellow theater kids. It never dawned on me that we might've been the weird ones at school, the artsy freaks, because I was having too much fun chugging Smirnoff Ice, scream-singing *Rent* and high on homoerotic straight bros. Plus, even if I wasn't the best singer, I loved doing it. I loved dancing, singing, acting, playing seventy-year-old creepy men one day and twinky Jet bottoms the next. I was good enough to keep getting roles, eventually even winning the Shuler Hensley Award for Best Supporting Actor in Georgia, and the praise of all this was currency enough to keep coming back to the stage.

My senior year of high school I directed a student run production of *The Sound of Music*. I invited my dealer and a posse of older gay men to show them what I'd created. They all came, and to this day, they still mention how powerful the show was whenever we run into each other. Naturally, this experience inflated my ego, and even if I didn't have all the chops to get into a strong musical theater conservatory, I was delusional and driven enough to make it to New York and push my way through Fordham's rigorous acting program.

Fordham provided me with the foundation I needed to begin taking the craft of acting not just seriously, but like the most important thing in the world. Following graduation, my plan was to continue studying at an MFA program. I sent off a slew of applications and auditions but didn't get in. Anywhere.

I was devastated. Was this really my path? Did I actually have what it took to be an actor? I spent most of my first year after Fordham in a kind of daze. I worked mornings at a coffee shop, then the rest of my day belonged to auditions. For eight months, nothing much happened, until *13 Reasons Why*. And all at once, everything changed.

Out of the blue, I got a call from the casting director. They wanted me to do a final—a chemistry read with Christian Navarro, who had already been cast as Tony, my character's love interest. If I wanted to participate, I needed to be in Los Angeles by 9:00 a.m. the following morning.

Holy fucking shit. I couldn't believe my luck.

I had already given up on getting the job, so when the call came, I knew I had to do whatever it took to make this thing happen. The flight was strange. I could tell when I boarded the plane that there were multiple other actors vying for spots on

13 Reasons Why, including for my role. They booked us all in the same two rows, just behind first class. Christina, this girl I knew from an acting class I was taking with Bob Krakower, was also auditioning. Seeing a familiar face helped calm my nerves. At least we were in this together.

I sat on the plane in my pajamas, hugging a tote bag filled with my outfit for the day: jeans, boots, and a tight mock-neck knit top from Zara. Just before the pilot made the announcement that we were landing, I shuffled into the tiny bathroom, changed into my outfit, quaffed my hair just so, and felt both emboldened by and terrified for the day to come.

I walked the long terminal at LAX, stopping in two different bathrooms on the way because otherwise the nerves would've had me shitting my pants. We each got in our own individual black SUVs—quite fancy—and were driven to the casting office. I was already told that we'd all be on red-eyes back home that evening, so there was no need to pack much beyond the essentials.

When I got to Barbara Fiorentino's office in Mid City it was two hours before my scheduled appointment time. They directed me to a Lemonade cafe, where I sat going over lines like a maniac until it was time for me to do the read. My competition for the role of Ryan were two actors named Cole Doman and Joey Pollari. There was also this guy in his early thirties who had recently done a musical I'd seen, but he was snotty, so I've mostly blocked him out of my memory.

The steepest competition, I felt, was between myself and Joey. Or maybe Cole because we looked so similar, which meant I also thought he was hot, because that's just how being gay is sometimes. Joey, however, already had a hit show that he was starring in, a limited series titled *American Crime* that one of the *13 Reasons Why* showrunners had worked on. When Brian Yorkey, the show's creator, came out to greet us before we went in, he had a familiarity with Joey that made me jealous. Nonetheless,

I reminded myself that there was no reason I couldn't land this job, even if I didn't have any legit credits on my résumé, and my IMDb was filled with made-up parts I'd played as extras in movies that were shot in Atlanta when I was in high school. (These have since been deleted.)

When I walked into the audition room, Christian gave me a massive hug. He'd gone to Rutgers with my friend and room-mate, Quinn, so I had messaged him on Facebook that I was coming to do a chemistry read, and he seemed excited. At least I had one fan in that room.

We did the first scene. It got some laughs. Tom McCarthy, the director and executive producer, wasn't there because he was busy directing the first two episodes, so Brian Yorkey gave me notes. I don't remember what they were, but something shifted, and when we did it again, it felt like I was flying.

I was asked to leave the room and wait to come back in to do the second scene. That's how they organized the callback process. Each of us went in a round. I was first, Joey second, Cole third, and that musical theater actor was fourth. It gave me enough time to have a glass of water and reorient myself but not enough to get irritated or psych myself out. I really spent a lot of time focusing on my "moment before" and my "moment after," trying to squish all the theater conservatory technique I could in these few pages. I was overly prepared for the audi-tion, and could've recited the lines backward and forward for all the characters. I also had been obsessed with Rachel McAd-ams's callback for *The Notebook*, and used it as inspiration for the breakup scene I had to do that day set in a coffee shop. I de-cided to pick up my bag and hold it on my shoulder like she did in her audition, walk out of frame, and then back into frame to deliver my last piercing final line. Tears ran down my face un-expectedly during that scene, and when we finished the work I saw that the creative team was crying as well. *That's probably a good sign, right?*

After the third scene, I thought I was done, but instead Brian threw something at us I still haven't experienced in any other audition. He wanted us to improvise, but it wasn't just any sort of improv. He handed me a Shakespeare sonnet, asked me to step out, familiarize myself with it, and come back into the room. His instructions were simple:

You're doing a poetry reading, you and Tony just broke up, and he walks in at some point in the middle. You can choose when.

And so I scribbled down the sonnet as quickly as I could in a notebook I had in my bag, as if it were my own. When it was my time to come back in, I grounded myself at an imaginary podium and introduced myself as Ryan Shaver, gave a name to the poem, and I started reading it. In some ways, it was like one of those nightmares where you suddenly find yourself on stage, except you're naked, but that kind of nervousness helped me. I took a few deep breaths, trying to force my feet to sink into the ground and read off the notebook because memorizing a sonnet in less than an hour wasn't going to happen. I didn't try to perform it in any epic way, just read it like I would read something in creative writing class in high school. I stumbled a bit, and checked in with my "audience" and, more than anything, I took my time. Christian graciously just made eye contact with me, intensely, and that moment opened the emotional floodgates, as I imagined seeing an ex-lover for the first time since breaking up. Bingo. I didn't have to do anything at all, it all happened for me. The gift of acting when it isn't forced is that, especially with good writing, the shit flows.

When I was finished, they thanked me for my time, and I was immediately shepherded back into one of the black cars.

Just before I hopped on my flight back to New York, I felt an incredibly strong urge to drink. Panicked, I called my sponsor and told her that I felt I might relapse. The pressure was just too overwhelming, and I was unbelievably anxious about what might happen. She assured me that wasn't the best solution, and offered me some prayers I could say on the flight. I repeated them in my head—the third step prayer from *The Big Book*—over and over again. I asked God in that moment to relieve me of the bondage of self. The rest of the flight I spent listening to *How Big, How Blue, How Beautiful* by Florence and the Machine on repeat. When I finally landed at JFK, I had a text message from my sponsor suggesting I call other alcoholics, ask them about their day, and get out of my self-obsession.

So I did. I stayed up all night calling other alcoholics I knew from the program, trying to distract myself. After that audition, I didn't hear anything for a couple of weeks, and again assumed that I hadn't booked the role. Then, on a beautiful June day, as I was sitting in a drive-through car wash in Keene, New Hampshire, with my fiancé, arguing about what rings we should get, I got a call telling me I'd booked the job and I had to be on the plane in forty-eight hours if I wanted to accept.

Was it luck? Was it destiny? Was it fate? Was God real? Thirteen was my lucky number, aligned with my birthdate, so perhaps my higher power was working for me the whole time.

Hardly two days later, I was in San Francisco to start shooting the first season. It felt like a dream. When I landed at SFO, memories of my ex-boyfriend Simon flooded through my brain. I remembered him picking me up from this exact terminal in high school, kissing me in his Audi A3 Sportback. *If only he could see me now...*

I felt like I had entered another universe, like I had time-jumped or quantum leaped. Whatever that saying is. Everything was so new, and I was too naive to care at the time about the fact that I was getting paid several orders of magnitude less than the rest of the cast, or that we were technically working overtime, or any of the other shit that I'm now hyperaware of when I'm working. The excitement of seeing trailers, soundstages, and costume fittings was enough. I could've died then and there, happy as a clam. I was also freaking out about meeting Selena

Gomez. She was executive producing the show, alongside her mother, Mandy Teefey, but was working remotely until the last few weeks of shooting.

I remember one night, after Selena took us out to dinner, she came back to hang with some of the cast at the hotel we were living in. The hours of laughter and play rolled on and when it was time to get her home we had to call an Uber for her as she didn't have the application on her phone. I remember thinking I'd be dead if we lost Selena-Fucking-Gomez to a serial killer Uber driver in the bay. As fate would have it, the driver who picked her up looked to be no older than 20, a beautiful girl with long brown hair, cruising in an older Toyota. Her face was pure shock, flushed beet red, when she saw Selena. Turns out she was a fan (shocking, I know) and an aspiring hairdresser. Wherever you are, girl, thanks for not getting us fired and getting mother home safely.

Every day, I showed up to set with a tingling in my stomach. It was a heady mix of emotions, at times extremely exciting, at times extremely nerve-wracking. My goal was always to simply do the best work I could, regardless of the circumstances. It was the most professional thing I'd ever been a part of, and I wanted to live up to the standards being set by all of the incredibly talented people around me: Greg Araki, Alisha Boe, Katherine Langford, Dylan Minnette, Miles Heizer, Devin Druid, Ross Butler, Brandon Flynn, and Michele Ang, among others. (Michele had been a year below me at Fordham. Just a few years prior she and I were in a terrible production of *Hedda Gabler* together, and now look at us!)

The second night I was in San Rafael; Brandon had the cast over at his place. Those of us who weren't series regulars stayed in a hotel off the freeway while the others were in apartments. When I got there, everyone was casually drinking. It felt like too much too soon to get into the sobriety of it all, so rather than field a million questions about why I didn't want a drink, I decided to simply decamp to the balcony for a cigarette. Within a few puffs, I looked over to find that Brandon had joined me. His boyish tipsy charm was intoxicating, he carried confidence with ease, and his blue eyes sparkled, perhaps this is what people meant when they said *star quality*. Whatever that was, Brandon embodied it. There was an undeniable charge between us when we locked eyes. We held each other's gaze for what felt like forever, and next thing I knew, we were up in his bedroom, ripping each other's clothes off. It was lusty and fun in the most beautiful, magical of ways. Three years sober I relished in the aftertaste of vodka on his tongue as it pushed against mine. Here I was, a *real* actor, filming a *real* show, hooking up with his *real* co-star.

Over the next few days, Brandon and I enjoyed a short-lived romance. He was open to something more serious, and I couldn't offer anything more than casual fun so eventually, he called it off. It was for the best; I needed to focus on my work while I was there anyway. He soon started dating Miles, at which point I started to wonder if I made a terrible mistake. Seeing Miles and Brandon so in love sparked an unexpected jealousy in me, a yearning for that excitement and fire, perhaps even more serious feelings lingered for Brandon at that time, but I couldn't do anything about it. My bed was made and I needed to focus on the task at hand: memorizing my lines.

While we were shooting the show, none of us really thought anyone would give a fuck about it when it came out. Netflix didn't have a history of successful teen shows at the time. We were the first. So when it did eventually see the light of day, and the world saw it for the tour de force it was, I was shocked. My socials started going crazy; I gained tens of thousands of followers practically overnight. I hadn't even come out publicly, yet there were already articles calling me a "gay icon" for reclaiming the word *faggot* on such a massive stage. I was flown to Milan to attend a fashion show, and signed with Anonymous Content, a large management company. We even presented as a cast at the MTV Awards. Suddenly, I had a stylist *and* a publicist.

What was this life?

When I knew that we were getting picked up for a second season, based on the runaway hit of season one, I felt an ease in my body for the first time: consistent work as an actor was hard to come by and there was no guarantee I would even return for season two, but luckily they made it clear that my character was essential to the storyline. I wasn't going to get bumped up to a series regular, though I didn't want to have to commute back and forth to New York for another six to eight months. So I convinced Peter that we should move to LA. Instead of flying from JFK to SFO multiple times a month, I only had to take a forty-five-minute regional flight up from LA. I was even able to cuddle my dog, Dabbs, on the weekends.

We couldn't really go around town like we did shooting our first season when we got back to the Bay. The Cuban restaurant we loved to eat at became flooded with fans whenever we showed up as a group. Over time, the attention started to affect each of us, albeit in different ways. During that second season, the cast split into smaller friend groups. I wound up sticking with the queers—Miles and Brandon—and their third, Alisha. We bonded over cigarettes, a love of RuPaul, and vintage shopping in the Castro. To be fair I was on the outside of all the formalized groups in the show since I came and went based on when I was working. Often coming back to the Bay Area was a whirlwind game of catch-up on what was happening. Usually though, I integrated easily into the social sandwich. Katherine Langford and I also got super close during that time as well and remain in each other's lives today.

Recently, the show came up on my Netflix suggestions. I hit play. It was the first time I'd watched since transitioning. I found myself having an almost out-of-body experience as I watched Ryan scheme his way across the screen. From where

I now stood, I so clearly saw a girl trapped within that cunty little gay, his bangs doing all they could to keep her from bursting out. At the same time, I was also proud of the work that I did. For a long time, I wrestled with my feelings over how I did on the show. As an actor, you're constantly evolving, and for several years after the show came out, I couldn't help but think about all the things I would do differently if given a second chance.

My career as an actor didn't take off quite in the way I'd hoped, but the fact that I'd built up a substantial online audience meant that I could support myself as I continued to relentlessly audition and work on screenplays. Commodifying my image hasn't come without its costs, though. That was the most "public" time in my life. I was constantly doing appearances, having my picture taken, blasting things out on the internet, far more often than I do now. This means that if you Google my name, the first image you're likely to see is one of me pre-transition. I've had to do a lot of therapy to get comfortable with the reality that I will never be able to erase my former body and self. It was immortalized on Calvin Klein billboards and the pages of magazines. On one hand I resent the success of my pre-transition self but on the other hand there's iconic memorabilia of my early twenties and I can see myself gathering my kids, grandkids, and showing them these photos—*look at what mommy used to look like!*

★ ★ ★

Even though LA was my primary residence for four years, I still like to pretend I didn't really live there; that it was just a home I kept shit in while I traveled and worked on projects in New York and Europe. I don't know why I feel such shame about it. The reality is, I did live there and for a while, I loved it. I loved having a home with a back and front yard; I loved living on the East Side and walking to Maru coffee in the mornings; I loved making Hollywood friends; I loved driving to Malibu on a random Tuesday to bake on the beach. In many ways, it was fab, and it served its purpose professionally. New creative connections lurked around every corner.

When the pandemic hit, though, and the city shut down, I quickly started to resent the relentless sun and began romanticizing the fact that there were seasons back on the East Coast. It was also the summer I began to medically transition, and my life in Los Angeles went further and further out of focus. As I approached one year on hormones and my marriage was officially dissolving, I knew there was nothing left for me in Los Angeles as a primary and permanent residence.

I fled back to New York to rediscover myself in the company of people who refused to make eye contact unless they knew you. I was no longer pretending to be a Silver Lake gay, perennially hot and happy and #lovinglife. For the first time, I was the real me—a *girl*—and as it turned out, this little ice queen had a penchant for the cold.

And I'd never once shivered in the California sun.

STRENGTH

upright: courage, bravery, confidence, compassion,
self-confidence, inner power

reversed: hedonism, self-doubt, lacking courage,
impulsivity, unsureness

A woman stands, confidently, petting the head of a lion. That's right, a fucking lion. My first thought is that I am a rising Leo, so perhaps this card does resonate with me. On the other hand, I don't feel particularly strong right now and I occupy spaces of self-doubt and impulsivity more often than confidence or power. There's an actor on this trip with us in Montana who towers over the group at six feet five inches tall. He walks in and out of spaces with a James Dean swagger and talks about his craft and personhood with radical assertiveness and clarity: he knows what he wants and goes for it, often winning in the end. It must be nice to just exist comfortably in your own skin and identity.

What exactly is strength? I see the power of motor boats cutting through the lake ahead of me, images of mothers giving birth to their infants flash before my eyes, a body builder lifting three times their weight above their heads, a downhill skier dominating moguls in the Olympics, my nephew taking his first steps—these are all examples of strength, at least physically. But what about mental strength? Chelsea Manning enduring solitary confinement? Living with the grief from a loved one passed? Pushing through bouts of suicidal ideation and depression? Sure. I suppose I can relate to the mental more than the physical because, though my body is healthy and suited for athletics, I cannot fathom pushing myself physically, like a marathon runner, because I would simply prefer to be horizontal as much as possible.

But moments and memories do flash in my psyche that remind me I am capable of strength—albeit often out of sheer necessity—but it's there. It might not be the first adjective I'd use to describe myself, but perhaps it isn't the last either. I often fail and fall on my face professionally or artistically and muster enough resilience to try again. I've always attributed that to delusion more than sheer strength, but then again that's my inner saboteur talking (a phrase my sponsor taught me early in sobriety). But still, without fail, I can think of moments in my life in which I stood tall and strong or did what was necessary to survive.

YOUTH

Can you tell us what happened today?

My mom's voice was quiet and quivering. I could feel the weight of the many eyes on me: my older brother Daniel's, my dad's, hers—all waiting in anxious anticipation for me to regale them with the trauma of the day. I was five, maybe six, and already found our family dinners boring because of this habitual questioning. We used to do a "rose" and "thorn" for the day, but recently it was all thorns. Instead of responding to her with words I anguished more and pouted, pushing my forehead into the wood-grained kitchen table we sat at for family meals. My grandfather, Ranger, made the table in the 1950s and he must've been a talented carpenter because it's still in use in my parents' kitchen today.

Driving my fingernails into my kneecaps, I stared at my brother's leg, which was shaking bombastically due to his restless leg syndrome, or more likely, undiagnosed ADHD. Every table fell victim to his habitual jitters. I didn't want to talk about what had happened that day because it wasn't any different than what happened every other day at my school, Woodland Elementary. My brother was in fifth grade; I was in kindergarten. He played on the basketball team and had more best friends than I had fingers and toes, whereas I pranced around school imagining I was a butterfly, until someone tripped me and laughed in my face. Most mornings, I would arrive on the bus eager to make a good impression. This hope was usually short-lived, though. Inevitably some asshole kid would make a comment about my pink clothes or princess backpack, and the day would be shot. By the time my parents picked me up, I'd have no more tears left to cry.

My feminine presentation and disposition as a biologically male kid was not understood by suburban Atlanta. I was a walking question mark. I shopped at Limited Too, wore flared bell-bottoms with flames on them, twisted my hair into braids, and skipped to class instead of walking. I idolized the Spice Girls and modeled my every aesthetic choice off their public personas. I was obsessed.

When Ginger Spice left the group, I didn't leave my room for days and I processed my grief by penning lengthy hate letters to her at their PO box—*You ruined my life! How could you break up the only thing that's ever mattered ever?!* I would beg for an explanation and for her to change her mind.

It's funny, my passion and affinity for redheads hasn't changed a lick since my adolescence. My wife is a redhead. Many of my ex-boyfriends are redheads. The girl I lost my virginity to in middle school, a redhead. Ginger Spice, wherever you are, you were probably my first love. So much of that music, emblematic of an era of girl power, was inspiring to me and in many ways, I felt their strength coursing through my veins when I blasted Spice Girls songs in my bedroom, choreographing silly little dances to them with friends, making home videos, and I'd bring that energy with me to school.

But it wasn't just the Spice Girls for me. I loved all things girly, which was fine when I was home because my parents were surprisingly chill about it. But days like this, when I would go to school dressed in short shorts and platform Doc Martens, with my hair set back in a sparkly headband, eyes would widen and laughter ensued. Those little Georgia peaches just didn't know *how* to respond.

Well, I guess some of them did. Some threw their backpacks into my face, filled with textbooks, scratching my cornea, or complained to teachers that my outfits were distracting. This happened on the school bus, in the cafeteria, in the halls, and was relentless.

The textbook to eyeball incident landed me in the doctor's office, and I had a pirate patch for a few weeks. As the school bus stopped in front of Woodland a much larger fourth grader clocked me with their Jansport. I burst into tears and felt the embrace of Daniel, my brother, who sat in the back of the bus with all his cool friends. That was the only year we spent at the same school, where I was safely in proximity to my older, revered brother.

I don't know what exactly happened to that particular bully, but I can imagine only the worst because my brother said he "took care of it." My brother, so tall and masculine, so tough he had pecs as a five-year-old. A jock in his youth, turned soft boy as an adult, a kind, well-mannered, cozy individual with so much strength for himself and strength to offer others. He sees the best in people, and he can also see the worst. While he didn't go out of his way to always support me as a kid, he never missed a moment to protect me during trials and was a fearless fighter.

But that evening, I didn't even know what to specify. I just stayed motionless praying for dinner to end so I could go to bed. In silence I waited for the conversation to switch tracks by scratching letters on the underside of the table, moving the wax between my fingernails.

I was tormented for simply existing in spaces that didn't know what to do with me, clearly triggering anger in my peers, and

I'd come home crying or pissed off, my light dimmed. My parents questioned me at the dinner table. At a certain point, the specifics became irrelevant. The who, where, and why didn't really matter because the offenses kept coming and my ability to defend myself, physically, verbally, was pretty much nonexistent. When someone went to throw a punch at me, I just took it, and then made my way to the nurse's office until someone came to pick me up.

Fighting back just wasn't my end game.

I preferred to stuff all the pain, misery, and fear in the back of my little brain and persevere. My silent protest was an unwavering commitment to being myself. That evening, my brother broke the silence: *Maybe you should stop dressing like a girl. Maybe that would help.*

And maybe he was right, but why should I? Why should I have to change how I exist for other people's comfort? While that distillation of intention wasn't available to me at the age of six, the essence of that feeling was instinctual and kept me alive back then. I gave up on school ever being the highlight of my day and reserved my joy for afternoons spent snacking on Lunchables at one of my few friends' houses. They were always girls, two of them named Lauren, and they treated me like kin. I idolized them all.

I don't want to do that, I finally said in response to my brother and nobody challenged me on it. Instead the family continued to respect my independence and lick my wounds. So every morning, without fail, I would just wear what I wanted to wear. Even when my parents tried to softly, or at times strongly, suggest more male-oriented clothing, I resisted. I didn't want to take their fear on as my own, and I could see how scared they were for me.

Eventually, my parents transferred me to a different school, one that would be more accepting of my quirks, called Paideia. Some of my older cousins went there and the school specialized in individualized learning. While there was less physical and outward violence directed toward me from peers and teachers, there was still a dissonance between us all, a void that I spent the remainder of my formative years trying to fill. I was pretty much the only boy who wore nail polish, apart from a kid named Lucas, who quickly became my only friend for the first year.

Meeting Lucas in the third grade was the first time I didn't feel unique. It was disorienting and comforting all at once. He showed me that I wasn't alone simply by sharing an affinity for nail polish and other girlier things. We started carpooling together and in the afternoons I would go home with his family and we would play hide-and-seek in laundry baskets and bins. This was a win for me and my parents who could finally breathe when I left in the mornings for school.

Lucas's older sister Ella was an eleventh grader at Paideia, and she had a belly button piercing I was enamored by. She was hot and confident and I was obsessed with her streaky highlighted bleached blonde hair.

From what I could tell, Ella didn't have a lot of friends, but the ones she did have were like family. She often talked about how bullshit high school was and how she couldn't wait to get the fuck out of Atlanta. That resonated with me. Even at that young age in third grade, I too felt like school was bullshit. I too wanted to get the fuck out of Atlanta. I just wanted to live in fantasy. I spent evenings praying to the universe to become a witch and be whisked away to Hogwarts.

My parents brought home a first edition of *Harry Potter and the Sorcerer's Stone* from a trip in London and my mom would read it to me every night to fall asleep. Eventually I started to pick up the reading portion because she often nodded out after a few paragraphs.

During my first year at Paideia most of my time in school was spent in my cousin Haley's classroom across the hall where I would brush her long, glossy brunette hair and get tips on where to get the most sparkly lip balm. She was, and still is, the kindest person I've ever known. She was my protector at the time, and I was grateful that the school let me just cuddle and nuzzle my way into her. Sitting on Haley's lap or braiding her long brunette hair was home for me.

As the years progressed, my claim to girlhood started to wane. Nobody explicitly forced me to change or present myself differently, but I could observe well enough how much ease and comfort came from aligning with your biological binary. In fifth grade, those years when hormones start to course through us, our puberty begins.

It dawned on me how much easier the boys had it, and it seemed like the girls who were girling could do so with ease by the time I made it to fifth grade. My peers were fitting into the societal expectations of their sex and genders, as many do when puberty starts and the hormones take over. By that time I decided that I would be a boy, whatever that meant, and when I got home from school on a Friday afternoon I piled all of my girls' clothing into a mountain on the driveway and lit it on fire.

Fuck being different, it was time for a new identity—I desperately needed a new era. I needed to be a boy.

Daniel and his friends came outside the house laughing and yelling in fear and excitement. *Badass, bro!*

As much as my brother let me be who I wanted to be as a kid, he shared in my exhaustion from sticking up for me to his friends who looked at me like I was an alien. The next day, I went with him and his buddies to the mall, and they helped me pick out boys' clothes. As my nanny at the time, Heather, described it, *I left on a Friday and you were a sweet kid. When I came back on Monday, you were a preteen asshole.*

Because I didn't have an innate organic male personality to lean into—I didn't love sports, I liked being more feminine and soft—I decided to transform into a male fantasy. My self-prescribed antidote to my transness as a child was simply mimicking and mirroring my older brother and his crew. I started to dress like them, talk like them, walk like them, treat girls like them, and it instantly worked. Within those first few days back at school, when people got over the shock that I was no longer wearing crop tops and writing exclusively with a pink gel pen, but instead wearing baggy skater clothes and hand-me-downs from PacSun, that I had transitioned from spending all my time at Claire's to Abercrombie & Fitch, that I started listening to Green Day and Fall Out Boy and punkier, louder music—I started to fit in.

Where before, I didn't have a lot of friends, aside from one or two similarly strange children, I was now on my way to being popular. I suppose, by and large, at least from the outside, I was a very attractive boy, and that evolved into being a pretty attractive teenager. My awkward phase, if there was one, didn't really inhibit me from making these new connections.

Within a month I had a girlfriend and started smoking weed; I became a rebel with a cause: don't be girly! That was my whole new persona, my whole new identity, and that became my strength. This version of myself that I could tap into. It was so liberating and way easier to have people adore me in those ways than constantly be at odds with society as a whole. I even played a season of basketball at the JCC just to prove how athletic I could be.

I started to make guy friends and leaned into more macho roles at ballet. It was the beginning of a new Tommy, a new version of myself. And whoever that girl was before, the one that was begging to get out, presenting in any way she could to be seen and heard and valued, well, she was fucking dead.

ESCAPE

I can't believe I'm typing this, but...do you know that famous Michael Jordan story? Like, the one where he got cut from his high school basketball team, only to become the greatest player of all time? My dad loves this story (read: every story about sports or businessmen or Buddhist monks who tweet). My brother even went to the Michael Jordan Camp for Basketball. So while I'm not necessarily an MJ fanatic, his meteoric and unprecedented rise to the top is seared into my brain cells. My family has kind of memorialized it and turned it into a myth that embodies a whole mess of ideological principles that are part and parcel of our worldview (and that of many Americans).

For starters, it illustrates that people are stupid. Like, how was that coach so blind that he couldn't see the raw talent that would barely half a decade later turn into the hottest young talent in basketball? But okay, maybe he needed to improve. Learn on the job, have a growth mindset, and #NeverGiveUp. Which brings me to my next point: namely, there are no handouts. You've gotta work hard as hell to get what you want. Nobody else cares about you and blah blah blah individualism. Michael knew this, and instead of crying and complaining, he kept grinding and grinding and grinding, and cemented himself as the greatest athlete of all time. And this is what ties it all together for us, because there is *nothing* we love more than a rags-to-riches story. Proof that the American Dream is real, that this really is the land of opportunity, and that as long as you're willing to put your nose to the grindstone, you, too, can become a baller.

Of course, anyone who's at least half paying attention knows this is bullshit. Not the Michael story, but what we glean from it. On a structural level, there's simply no such thing as the American Dream. I mean, this is obvious to anyone who made it through, I don't know, elementary school. It isn't dead, it just never existed. Plus, on an individual level, I think concepts like "strength" and "resilience" are highly contingent upon myriad factors, notably the context in which your adversity and hardship is taking place.

In this way, I find it hard to talk about myself as being "strong." I could probably write down a million adjectives to describe myself before that word ever even entered the general conversation. In my experience, this is actually quite common— most people struggle to envision themselves as genuinely capable of pushing through hardship. In my own life, I've always viewed it as something more akin to an episode of *Wipeout* where the contestant is getting their shit rocked, but still somehow managing to stay out of the water. Like, I'm not really in control, but somehow it's working out.

Yet my "strength" and "courage" seem to be about the only thing others can agree are definitely there when it comes time to take stock of what's in my emotional fridge. Especially once I became open about the fact that I'm trans, it seemed almost inescapable.

Sure, being trans in the public eye takes guts. That's why it took me so long to share my truth with the world. Honestly, I didn't really feel like it was anybody's business, and I'd be lying if I said my decision to come out as trans didn't have a whole lot to do with pragmatic considerations related to my career and mostly tiring of coming out to people individually. Ripping the Band-Aid off and having my own gender reveal party for the public was a compact way to step into my new life.

The older I get, though, the more I acknowledge that a similar murkiness clouds the water of every act of apparent courage. Nobody is ever all brave; nobody is ever all bad; nobody is ever all anything, but we all are capable of being everything. We're like the undulating waveforms of a song, rising and falling, rising and falling, rising and... Sometimes courage peaks while fear falls; sometimes they rise in equal measure; sometimes there's just stillness. The presence of courage doesn't mean the absence of other complex emotions. What else do you have to be strong in the face of if not your own fear?

Perhaps, then, it's more appropriate to think of strength not as one's ability to endure, but to give certain frequencies a little more—or less—juice. In this sense, it took a lot of equalizing to get to where I am, to become someone whom I love and respect. To become right sized after a lifetime of oscillating violently between low-lows and high-highs.

For a long time indeed, a life of professional success and personal fulfillment seemed all but impossible. Which brings us back to the Michael Jordan of it all, because I've got an MJ story of my own. To tell it, though, we have to go back to when I was just a nine-year-old goofball who wore flamed bell-bottoms to school (they are exactly what they sound like, denim bell-bottoms embellished with embroidered flames that come from the bottom to the knee).

I was in the fourth grade, and our big class project that year was to make ourselves time capsules. The mandate was for us to leave them untouched until we graduated from high school. The main idea was to think about who we'd be in a decade's time, and how the world around us might have changed. (That

9/11 occurred shortly thereafter was lost on no one.) To give the whole thing a visual metaphor, we were also instructed to make a drawing of what our nine-year-old selves anticipated our eighteen-year-old selves would look like, and stick it to the top of the capsule.

Fast-forward nine years, and I fudged the rules a bit. To my credit, though, I was sad, and I felt like the only proper course of action was to make myself even sadder. So a few days before graduation, I pulled the slightly rusted lunch box out of my closet, took one look at it, and began to sob. This was mostly the self-portrait's fault, because it hit me like a fucking freight train.

The draftsmanship wasn't stellar, but that made it all the more powerful, all the more devastatingly raw. This chicken scratch version of Tommy was a bad bitch. She was a defiant dyke. Her shoulders were arched back, accentuating her chest and rendering her silhouette an invitation to all manner of unspeakable things. What's more, she was covered in tattoos, practically begging you to step to her, to try to knock her down, to hurt her. She couldn't be touched.

Because she was strong.

Life, however, was not imitating art. This was a time in which things were not particularly positive, or grounded, or just generally healthy for me—and I had nobody to blame but myself. There was only one thing in the world that truly brought me joy—that allowed me to feel a zest for life—and that was theater. I was heavily involved in musical theater, and by my senior year, I was directing the student-run show, and even though I showed up to the first rehearsal still high on my drag-queen-drug-dealer's cocktail of 2cB, Molly, and god knows what else, it was a hit.

My hippie lib school was big into the performing arts. It was an upside-down world where male leads were cool as fuck, and jocks got made fun of for, I don't know, being sweaty. When it came to acting, I was one-track minded: Broadway or bust. More traditional acting programs, like Tisch or Juilliard or Carnegie Mellon, weren't even on my radar. My dream school was Elon in North Carolina, which felt far enough away that I could feel like I was starting something new, but still close enough that I could drive home to lick my wounds if needed. (And yes, it is where Taylor Trensch went, who at the time was Broadway's preeminent gay wunderkind; I was only mildly obsessed with him.)

As much as I loved performing, however, I couldn't manage to prioritize it over my more immediate, indulgent impulses, which were, among other things, railing lines of blow while getting railed by men twice my age. It seemed like everyone else had a guidebook for living, and I hadn't been handed a copy. Science makes it pretty clear that when we're in pain, it's nigh on impossible for us to think in the long term. Instead, we're damned to drift from one hollow decision to another, none of them bringing us the happiness or fulfillment we're so desperately in search of.

This is the vicious cycle I was stuck in, and it led to incessant partying, a complete lack of inhibition, and a 2.7 GPA. My SAT scores didn't do me any favors either. I took it right at the end of junior year, which also happened to coincide with grad party season. I stayed out until 6:00 a.m. the night before taking Jägerbombs at Felix's, high on Molly dancing atop a pool table. Naturally, I couldn't let the comedown hit midtest, so I was constantly asking to go to the bathroom to take key-bumps. Anyone with half a brain would have justifiably assumed I was cheating—until they saw my score. I didn't bother retaking the test.

As a result of all of this, I got rejected from all fifteen of the musical theater programs I applied to. Thus, Michael Jordan.

(Yes, it sounds a lot less sexy than MJ's thing. I concede that. But at the time, it felt absolutely catastrophic.)

To make matters worse, the same day I opened up my time capsule, I'd been informed that I would no longer be allowed to perform at my graduation ceremony. Why? I missed rehearsal.

Why did I miss rehearsal? I stayed out until 6:00 a.m. the night before taking O-bombs at Felix's, on enough Molly to make Aubrey Plaza crack a smile. Once more, the only thing standing between me and my dreams was…me.

If you've ever known a theater kid (or perhaps are one yourself, which is honestly the likelier scenario if you're reading this book), you can imagine how this much rejection would cause them to lose their mind.

And that's kinda what I did.

The last month or so of high school is a black hole—or maybe a black box filled to the brim with absolute depravity. I went buckwild. One of the few memories I actually have is of telling a group of friends that I simply hadn't applied to any colleges, and that was why I didn't know where I was going yet. To this day, thinking about this makes my cheeks flush, causes my pulse to quicken, my stomach to tighten, and a deep-seated sense of shame to take root.

But the truth was I did know where I was going: Columbia College, in Chicago.

A quaint private art school in the city's South Loop neighborhood, Columbia is actually quite a good place to develop your craft. I was able to get in academically, and on top of that, you didn't have to audition to participate in the theater program.

When I showed up to campus in the fall, the only thing I had going for me was the arrogant belief that I was better than this place. Actually, that might not be the right way to phrase it. I should say I had a "strong will," because honestly, I was pretty frickin' humbled, and my desire to do better actually made me *less* confident, like I was an outsider by virtue of being *too* inside.

I couldn't tell you what my dorm looked like, or what the names of the people I hung out with were, but within a few days, I'd made friends with all the other addicts; by orientation, we were in the auditorium munching ecstasy pills like they were popcorn.

A few days into the semester, I auditioned for the main stage musical, a production of *Floyd Collins*. (Truly a beautiful piece of art, especially if you like haunting, folk inspired music.) I got cast in the chorus, which doesn't sound like much, but was actually pretty impressive given that I was a freshman, and out of three hundred auditions, only thirty people got a spot.

Okay, I said to myself, *maybe this won't be all dog shit after all.*

But then rehearsals began. I don't know how to explain this without coming across as conceited, or aloof, or in any other way that doesn't make me seem like a total bitch, but the fact of the matter was that I was heads and shoulders above almost everyone. I'd been doing ballet since I could walk, classical voice training since sixth grade, and attended a school with a very well-funded arts program. If I *wasn't* at least somewhat ahead of my peers at Columbia, it'd be a pretty damning indictment of both myself and my training.

Normally, someone with my performance background would have been gunning for one of the aforementioned prestige schools. They would have made sure their grades weren't a limiting factor. They'd have enjoyed a good night's sleep before all of their auditions, and they most certainly wouldn't have shown up catastrophically hungover, causing them to have panic attacks on stage and forget their lines.

But I wasn't one of those people. I'd fumbled the bag of my own privilege, failed to take advantages of the tremendous opportunities I'd been afforded, and now I found myself in the back row of a chorus full of singers that, to be frank, I likely wouldn't have even cast as Sister Sophia in my production of *Sound of Music*. And it wasn't because I didn't have the talent or fortitude to forge a career in entertainment. It was simply because I hadn't been responsible.

I know all of this must sound terribly cruel, but the reality of the performing arts is that you either have it or you don't, and while lots and lots of expensive training won't guarantee you have it, it goes a long way in making sure you don't *not* have it.

A few weeks into the semester, I was scheduled to meet with my advisor, who also happened to be my acting teacher. I'd taken a couple pills the night before, and was feeling pretty empty when I plopped down in front of his desk. I distinctly remember feeling like I was going to sink into the cushion because it was so worn down, and desperately hoping that this would come to pass. I did *not* want to be there. I was expecting him to go through the motions, to ask me some canned questions about how everything was going and what my long-term plans were. Instead, he offered me a polite smile, then shook a paper at me.

I'll be honest, he said. *We don't usually see students like you at Columbia.*

What do you mean? I asked.

He chuckled.

Well, typically people with your experience and, to be forthright, talent opt for programs that are a bit more rigorous and that have more of a national profile. Are you feeling challenged here?

I sat up in my chair, intrigued. I'd never heard such affirming words from someone in his position before. On a conscious level, I'd been telling myself I was "better" than everyone else, but deep down, my biggest fear was that I truly wasn't—that even worse than failing to make good on my potential, I'd never had any in the first place. His words, brief though they were, soothed my soul like a warm bowl of chicken noodle soup. They opened me up, softened me for the first time in months, maybe years.

I...thank you, I managed to stammer. *I had a bit of a unique high school experience.*

He studied me, tapping his fingers on the desk in a rolling trill.

I'd never discourage a student from being here at Columbia. It's a wonderful place full of wonderful people. But it's not for everyone, and if you feel you might fall into that category, I'd be happy to help you consider some alternative courses of action.

I ran home from that meeting and immediately began doing all of the things I should have been doing four years earlier. Still, I'd accepted—at least on some level—that I was stuck at Columbia College, even as I maintained an ardent belief that I would be a "star."

It's right about now that I should probably introduce you to Simon, reddish blond bangs mopped on a freckled forehead providing shade to his Tiffany-blue eyes. Arguably my first love, he and I had a relationship that was defined by its tumult and turbulence (from both parties). That said, during this time in my life, he was the only thing keeping me from going absolutely insane. He was attending George Washington University in DC, and we'd frequently fly out to stay with each other, often acting on pure impulse. Like, one minute I'm getting drunk in the South Loop, and the next thing I know, I'm stepping off the plane at Dulles.

Without him, I never would have realized that transferring schools was a real possibility. I figured I'd made my bed, and now I was going to have to lie in it.

What do you mean you have to lie in it? Simon asked.

We were in my little twin bed, both reeking of each other's bodies. He propped his head up with his left hand and I lit a cigarette. His expression made clear that he thought I was a fucking idiot.

Fuck that. Just transfer.

I shrugged.

What college is gonna take me? I have a 2.7 GPA.

He shook his head, smiled.

Had a 2.7 GPA. But now you have a clean slate. You can just, like, use your grades from Columbia. I wanna get out of DC anyway. Maybe we can both go to NYU.

This sounded way too good to be true. Simon wasn't one to

lie, but he also spoke in lullabies and musings from time to time. A child of divorce with creative parents in the Bay Area, he held a capacity for daydreaming and wistfulness that felt both comforting and unnerving at once. Sensing my skepticism, he pulled out my laptop and Googled something like *does high school GPA matter transferring colleges*. We read through several articles about the process, and I was shocked that he was right. Not universally so, but for my purposes, I wouldn't need to use my high school transcripts.

If it wasn't already clear, this whole transferring business was made possible by a tremendous amount of privilege. To begin with, I'd gone to an exceptionally good high school, which had, in spite of all my chicanery, prepared me well for the rigors of college. This meant that even though I was still using heavily, I was able to maintain a 4.0 GPA my first semester at Columbia, primarily due to the fact that I was simply used to managing a more intense workload than what their curriculum demanded.

On top of this, I also had the financial means to be able to travel to New York to tour the schools I was looking at. This meant that I was able to put careful thought (at least, as careful of thought as my nineteen-year-old addict mind would allow for) into where I saw myself thriving aka partying aka fucking my hot boyfriend who looked like me.

Originally, I'd been enamored with the idea of going to NYU Tisch. It felt sexy and prestigious, and the thought of being a Village girl was so romantic it made my heart want to explode. On the same trip that I visited NYU, however, I also swung by Fordham at the behest of Simon. He'd had a friend who really wanted to study theater there, so he knew quite a bit about the program.

Hardly fifteen minutes into the tour, I was enamored. As we walked through the windowless ground floor (which somehow made me feel safe, even though in theory, it should've been wildly claustrophobic) in which the program lived, I was stunned by how diverse and multifaceted the student body was.

Everybody there was passionate about their craft. The program only accepted sixteen students each cycle, affording the teaching a level of intimacy—and the performances a level of competitiveness—that I'd desperately been craving. As a ballet girl, succeeding without competition in a semi-suffocating environment wasn't possible. On top of that, the curriculum also incorporated elements of a traditional liberal arts education, which I was attracted to. I didn't want to be an actor who couldn't do their research. Plus, the place was crawling with faggots—both students and faculty and most importantly, at the law school. The fact it was a Jesuit institution didn't mean fuck all—at this point my half-Jewish ass was determined to fill a seat.

There was only one catch: at the end of the tour, they told me I couldn't transfer until my sophomore year—and this was in October of my first semester. I remember feeling my face flush, my eyes beginning to sting as they filled with tears.

And this is where strength comes in. Or maybe delusion. Again, fine line. The fact of the matter was that, in my mind, the decision was already made: I was *not* going to spend another semester at Columbia. I just needed to convince someone at Fordham that I was special enough to skip the line.

Again, I can't stress enough just how feral I was for getting the hell out of Columbia, and as the tour wound to an end, my mind was racing as it tried to come up with any plausible means of showing them who I was and why I deserved to be there yesterday. For better or worse, only one plan came to mind. That plan was, essentially, to cause a scene.

At the time, the director of the theater program was a man named Martin Maple. He had the air of a well-trained actor, the kind of Shakespearean gravitas that just oozes out of someone that has it, but a reserved understanding that his time for fame or flowers or fortune had ultimately passed. His power was clawing into college kids' souls and basking in the glory of tenure. Thanks to the tour, I knew where his office was, and once everyone had dispersed, I practically sprinted over and rushed right in.

He was sitting calmly at his desk, and I recall him giving me a look like, *This ought to be interesting.* Still, he gave me a warm welcome and allowed me to say my piece. So I did.

Martin, I'm suffocating in Chicago.

He looked startled. *That sounds dramatic. What about your school isn't working for you?*

I saw this as a test, like would I shit talk or would I offer them credit where it was due.

It's not that the school is a problem, the faculty is kind, and the classes aren't baseless...it's just that I'm not challenged enough there. And hearing you and the other students talking about this program, I know I'm supposed to be here. Plus, who wants to be on central time anyway? It's annoying for everybody.

He chuckled at this. A win.

I used this time to paraphrase the banner I saw above the escalator on the way to the cafeteria, giving my best Elle Woods, *I want Fordham to be my school and New York to be my campus. I want to be around other actors. I want to be challenged. I can't be the best person in my program as a freshman. I want to be the next John Benjamin Hickey or—*

He went here, you know. Before Juilliard.

Duh, dipshit. I Googled it. *No way! See, kismet...*

His brow suddenly furrowed in a way that was emotionless, like he was being pulled backward down the long hallway of his brain, waiting for a door to open with the right response. Finally, his spell broke, and he made direct eye contact in the way actors or teachers of children do that signaled: listen to me.

Your passion is clear. Why don't you record an audition tape and send it over, and if accepted, we'll see what we can do to get you in for the spring semester.

I nearly passed out.

I'm sure in his mind, there was no chance in hell I was getting in. He was satiating me, surely. Some rando from a mediocre program in Chicago barging in on him unannounced and proclaiming their worthiness? I sometimes wonder how many came before. Like, was I just the latest in a long line of melodramatic thespian queers begging at his altar?

Whatever the case, I hit the ground running in Chicago, wasting no time rounding up my transcripts and securing recommendations from my professors, who were extremely kind about the whole transferring business. Much to my surprise—and delight—I was accepted on academic grounds almost immediately, which meant all that was left was for my audition to be considered.

In the meantime, my first semester at Columbia College spiraled to an end, and I schlepped back to Atlanta with bated breath and a hangover. That whole holiday season, the only thing I could think about was whether or not Martin Maple would get the last laugh. Not that he didn't want me to come to Fordham, just that the only logical reaction to having someone profess their worthiness to you in such a dramatic fashion, only for their audition to prove that they are anything but, would be to, like, fucking lol.

So I waited…and waited…and waited. Waiting in bathhouses and after-parties, waiting while smoking cocaine with drag queens after hours in East Atlanta, waiting while burning through a carton of Camel Crushes. The break seemed to move at a glacial pace, and by New Year's, I was losing my goddamn mind. It was the first time I'd ever done a classical monologue, and a not so small part of me wondered if I even had the chops to pull it off. I rewatched my audition video ad nauseam. What if instead of rescuing me from a place I felt I wasn't meant to be, all these shenanigans were simply going to prove once and for all that I was a flop?

As if things could get even spicier, my parents had no idea I was doing any of this. Over the break, anytime they asked why I was pulling my hair out or chewing my nails down to the nub, I'd shrug and say, "School." I imagine this probably sounds silly to you. Why not enlist the help of my parents? Wouldn't that make things easier?

On some level, maybe. The fact that I was even at Columbia, however, was a boondoggle of my own creation, and though I'd never have admitted it at the time, I was ashamed of myself. I didn't want to drag anyone else into the process of undoing what felt like (to me at least) a massive fuckup, least of all my parents. I'm speaking with the clarity of hindsight, of course. At the moment, none of this was really running through my head. I was acting on pure instinct, and my instincts said leave my parents the hell out of this.

Thus, they were perplexed when I hardly said a word before flying back to Chicago for spring semester. I still hadn't heard back from Fordham, and my days began to be characterized by a latent sense of dread. Arriving back at campus, I could feel my throat closing up. How the fuck had I managed to screw this up? The only glimmer of hope I had was the fact that Fordham didn't start classes until two weeks after Columbia, which meant there was still time—but precious little.

Rehearsals finally began for the production of *Floyd Collins* I'd been cast in at the beginning of the year. I distinctly recall feeling like I was hallucinating throughout the duration of our first vocal session, and not just because of the ketamine I'd snorted. Because certainly this couldn't be my life, right? It *must* be someone else's, no? Could it really and truly be me singing "'Tween a Rock an' a Hard Place" next to someone who at the beginning of the rehearsal told me he had no idea who Duncan Sheik was? Impossible.

During the fourth rehearsal, I was practicing harmonies with a few other chorus girls when I felt my phone vibrate. More annoyed than anything, I took it out to turn off my notifications, only to see that I'd received an email. From Fordham. I was instantly hit by a serious case of the tummy tingles. I looked up at my castmates, tried to bring them into the moment so I wouldn't have to shoulder all of the anxiety alone. They just kinda stared at me, though, like, *Why is this bitch so bent about the sixteenth measure of "How Glory Goes"?*

I opened the email, saw I was in, and immediately put down my songbook and left. I don't remember exactly how I made my exit, but it was no doubt abrupt. Something to the tune of, *It's been great, y'all, but I'm out. Bye!*

It didn't take me long to pack my bag. (Yes, *bag*, in the singular.) I don't think I'd even put anything up on the walls. All I really had were some clothes and a dwindling supply of drugs. I remember sitting on my bed and looking out the window at the snow-laden Chicago streets. For the past few months, the sight of snow had depressed me, made me feel like a frozen figure in a snow globe; but now there was something hopeful about the flurries as they tossed about in the wind. For the first time, I noticed that Chicago was actually quite charming. Had the view from my dorm always been this...pretty? It's amazing how your perception of reality can change when you don't feel like you're drowning.

There was really just one last thing to do before I hopped on a flight to New York, and that was to take care of the very small, super minor, and totally inconsequential matter of telling my parents what I'd done. Again, I'd been acting on such raw emotion that I hadn't really had time to consider how they might react. I'd done my homework on all the finances, so I knew it wasn't going to cost them anything more for me to transfer, but this meant nothing as far as the real meat of the move was concerned. Would they approve of me uprooting my life in the span of twenty-four hours? Would they be angry with me for having done all of this right under their noses? In considering these questions, self-doubt slowly set in. Shit, *was* this the right move? *Had* I been insane to do this? Was this little more than the erratic, illogical behavior of an addict?

These are thoughts that were haunting me as I dialed my dad.

Hey, T.

As soon as I heard him say my name, my voice caught in my throat.

H-he-um, hi... Dad.

Everything okay? He laughed, teasing me.

I took a deep breath, looked back out the window at the intensifying snowfall. I reminded myself that I was on the other side, and I just needed to give him the good news.

So I closed my eyes, swallowed hard, and told him everything.

When I finally finished explaining myself, he was silent. I could hear the rasp of his breath through the line, could picture exactly the face he was making as he considered what he'd just heard—eyes faintly squinted, head slightly cocked, lips gently pursed.

After what felt like forever, he finally spoke.

You really ran into the dean's office like that?

The question caught me off guard.

Well, I—yeah. Basically.

The line got fuzzy as it struggled to relay his boisterous laughter.

Ah, hell, T. I mean what can I say? Honestly, I'm impressed. You went out and you did it. You knew what you wanted and you wouldn't take no for an answer.

Really?

Really. Do you have a place to live in New York?

I'm gonna figure that out.

Well, if you can get there and you can find a place to live, then your mom and I aren't gonna stand in the way and tell you no. This is your life; it's your story you're writing. You have to tell it in the way that feels right to you.

He paused. I wondered if that was a Thich Nhat Hanh quote or from a Hallmark card.

I'm proud of you. This took guts.

Did it? Throughout the whole process, I'd been so desperate

to get out of Chicago that I don't think fear or courage factored much into the equation. Hearing my dad say this, though, I couldn't help but get a little choked up. I'd spent so long wondering if I wasn't a massive fuckup, if I had any talent whatsoever, if there was anything even remotely redeemable about me at all, that such words of affirmation—especially from my dad—were like a punch in the gut. A good punch, but one that knocked the wind out of me nonetheless. And yes, there was still the matter of my addiction to tend to, but for the moment, the only thing I could think about was celebrating this victory.

Thank you, Dad.

Of course. I love you, T. Give 'em hell in New York.

I love you, too. And I will.

We hung up, his words lingering in the frigid air.

I'm proud of you. This took guts.

You bet your ass I began to sob.

I didn't really have any loose ends in Chicago. I hadn't made any particularly deep connections, either with people or places (aside from our Idina Menzel king, may he live long and prosper), so it felt pretty easy to put a bow on that chapter of my life.

During the ride to O'Hare, I remember taking in the Chicago skyline and trying to make sense of what the past six months had been, how it would slot into the grander narrative of my life. It had felt so long, but in truth, six months was hardly a blip. Was this actually strength, or was I simply running from my problems?

Before these feelings could really take on a life of their own, though, we pulled up at the departure curb, and all I could think about was how excited I was to finally be on my Blair Waldorf shit.

The rest, as they say, is history.

It's at this point in a normal book that I'd make much ado about how I learned and grew from that experience. I'd make a meal about all the things it taught me, and how this was a pivotal crossroads in my life, and I managed to make the right choice and so on and so on and so on.

The truth is that I was flying by the seat of my pants when I transferred. Yeah, I was motivated, but in reliving this story, I realize now just how amorphous that motivation was. Was it courage? Was it fear? Was I just fucking annoyed? The most likely answer is a mix of all three.

I wasn't all brave; I wasn't all bad; I wasn't all anything; and I definitely didn't walk away from Chicago with some newfound clarity or deep insight into the nature of my being.

Strength is something different. It finds its form in the mundane. The trick, I think, is simply to become aware of that, to recognize that even the weakest of flops is imbued with hints of a slay. It's embracing imperfection, embracing weakness, giving the middle finger to the patriarchal ideal of "manning up" and just letting yourself cook.

With all of this in mind, would you believe me if I told you that Michael Jordan didn't actually get cut from his high school basketball team? Because he didn't. He just didn't make varsity as a sophomore. He was still on the JV team. This is well-documented. Michael has admitted on multiple occasions that he needed to improve certain areas of his game, and he also just wasn't big enough yet. He kept practicing, as did most of his peers, and a year later, made varsity. This one slight didn't offer him the spiteful motivation he needed to dedicate himself to the singular pursuit of becoming the greatest basketball player of all time. No, he was just like, *Fuck. I gotta keep getting better.* And in the ensuing year, he thought about a lot of other shit than basketball, and he felt a lot of other things than anger at the thought of being cut (mostly because, again, he *wasn't* cut).

But this doesn't make for a good story.

THE NOMINEE
PART II

I wonder sometimes if I'm just an exploration for you. Like a land you could never travel alone, I hold the key to some portal you wish to call home. A lost alien trying to find your way back to your planet, you spotted me and felt the opposite of a gravitational pull. Like maybe your wings had been clipped somewhere in the woods of Montauk as a child, and as a result, you've spent decades trying to decode this thing called life. Trivial, triumphant, tremendous.

The way you tuck your hair behind your ears hurts me.

I used to wonder how a person could cry and laugh in the same breath until I met you. I've never been so unsure in my life, walked so heavy on eggshells, tiptoed into different forms of being to please someone. I've never wanted to impress someone more than I want to impress you.

I envy the space you take up, you energetic redheaded giant.

You're on your own planet, planet Narcissus. I wish you could see yourself the way that I do. So fabulously stunning and demure. And vicious, cruel, unnerving, too. When you check in with me, I wonder if it's because you've been taught to ask these types of questions.

And so I must ask myself why I'm here. What is our purpose? Why do I feel an insatiable desire to define it for us? The tenor of your voice perforates my body.

Lovesickness never made sense until I met you and I wonder every day how someone could survive a lifetime of this. Holding on for dear life.

So I wonder now, as I watch you across from me in Mexico City, pacing on your own planet, can I replace this feeling of fear with gratitude. Can I just enjoy the moment as I have it, and hold the space that I need to remember your smell and taste and touch, however fleeting. Can I just for once in my life not concern myself with the need to define what this could be or has to be when it doesn't have to be anything at all.

And I never knew *smell* before you. Only shelf-bought fragrance blended with skin, enhanced by deodorant or bad breath. Cigarette smoke or sweat, but never your unique musty scent. I've never felt jealousy like this before. You smile at someone else and it terrifies me.

I can't shake the feeling we're meant to be. Just maybe not on this planet or in this life.

Every expectation I could've had of you has been flipped upside down and maybe that's why I love you so fucking much, like I'd jump in front of a train for you kind of love. A stupid sickening sour kind of love. Untamable, confusing and contradictory kind of love.

A love that leads to hate.

A fuck you kind of love.

A BROKEN HEART

After my relationship with The Nominee blew up I didn't know how to process my grief. On the one hand, I wanted him to burn and die and on the other hand I wanted to be held by him. Neither of which were feasible options and both felt like losing. I blocked and deleted his number and thanked God he didn't have a social media presence. This didn't stop me from searching his name on Twitter obsessively to see where he was spotted and make sure I wasn't anywhere near. Instead of a burn book devoted to him, I took to my notes app to vent because what else is a girl to do when grieving the loss of an emotionally manipulative and abusive ex all on her own? Perhaps this was karma for how I treated Peter…

September 12th, 2021

I wanna take time to thoughtfully and intentionally process what's transpired so when we talk next I can do it from the clearest space. I'd like to suggest we take a week off—no texting, calling, seeing each other. If we want to communicate something we write it down.

September 9th, 2021

Your actions don't match your words; I feel that you're deeply manipulative and self-involved.

You text me with little regard.

Falling in love for the first time as a trans girl at twenty-nine is embarrassing.

What's wrong with me?

September 28th, 2021

I'm sorry that you're having such a hard time. This has become a really vulnerable and painful space for me, so at this moment I'm going to step back for a while.

Wishing you the best. I love you.

August 9th, 2021

Sometimes youth makes it really hard not to be a narcissist—and I hope that you recognize you have real work to do because that will only deepen if you don't go to a real therapist instead of equine therapy from a half-blind woman over zoom.

You use all this therapeutic language to mask the fact that you don't have any empathy for me. Your literal behavior lacks empathy.

July 5th, 2021

I need space but I don't know how to ask for it.

November 5th, 2021

The day I met you I knew you'd break my heart. It was the kind of love nobody could withstand. My brain turned into a million pieces of Dippin' Dots, sticking to one another, melting into mush when I thought of you. Strawberry flavored. The sheer glance you gave me through ginger eyelashes in the rain outside of Books Are Magic sent a wave of fear from my toes to the tip of my pelvis and through the roof of my head. Holding your gaze was impossible for me; you saw into my soul. It was terrifying. How could I compete?

I thought I needed you more fully in those moments than I needed air. What I needed was an escape.

Memory is a funny thing, how it can wipe itself clean of responsibility, bad behavior, and what most would call blaring siren red flags or triggers; tips that you were and still are emotionally abusive.

Memory wants to hold on to four lustful months, three impulsive weeks in Mexico, two fucks on the beach, and one inflamed heart—a heart that is sore from your punches, a body aching from being yanked around like your puppet—and turn it into *The Boy Who Got Away.*

But I can't forget the bad things. I have to force my brain to hold on to them, lest I forget and fall into your hands again like weightless prey…the bad things like you wielding therapeutic language to mask the fact that you don't have any empathy for me. The bad thing like forcing me to watch you play with my shit in the toilet when I wanted to run away. The bad thing like you kept fucking me when I asked you to stop. The bad thing like you pretending to be trans like some shitty Vegas Strip version of Daniel Day-Lewis.

June 8th, 2021

Am I an experiment for you? Or a collectible? Like the first trans girl in the trans girl menagerie you're curating?

October 1st, 2021

Honestly, [Redacted]: fuck you. You used me. The fact that you put me through this is incredibly narcissistic and sociopathic. I will never forgive you.

July 17th, 2021

I'm at a loss. This week has been a blur in so many ways; an attempt to reckon with unbelievable circumstances. I don't like being angry at you, as I have been. I'm really hurt and confused and exhausted. Can you just walk me through what happened?

Did you ever love me?

Did I do something wrong?

I feel used by you, like an experiment not a human being. I can't believe that you ever loved me, just the idea of me. The hardest thing is that I don't know what actually happened, what I did or didn't do, what transpired and led to you treating me so cruelly.

You will likely continue to treat people like shit behind a therapist's facade of self-protection that is all a long-winded way of saying you're a fucking coward.

But people need to know to stay away from you. Trans women need to know to stay away from you. You tortured me at my most vulnerable moment.

You might be the cruelest person I've ever known. I wanted so badly to believe you weren't like this. And yet, you continue to prove otherwise. I had faith for a brief moment that you would be open to one last phone call, and yet—not much to my surprise—you aren't. You're just a sad coward who preyed on a vulnerable trans girl.

September 16th, 2021

I can't believe you dropped my shit off in the hotel lobby in a Sweet Green bag you fucking coward.

November 8th, 2021

I'm not angry at you, you don't know better.

What is there to even be angry about?

Now I ask: How can I grow?

Because... At the end of the day, it is what it is.

And all I have is today, and I can say for certain a few things:

I am safe, I am contained, and I can process the feelings.

I'm finding gratitude to oppose my self-pity.

I'm sober.

I have a good, healthy body. I have Covid but it could be worse, I'm fighting this fucked-up virus.

November 27th, 2021

Honestly, [Redacted], forget I even asked. I was hoping to find a brief moment to see each other in an effort to avoid running into you in New York unexpectedly and curb some of my fear and anxiety from the PTSD I have as a result of your manipulation and emotional abuse of our entire relationship. I was hoping that if it was planned, since the former is inevitable, maybe it would be more bearable and do less harm.

But, not surprisingly, your willingness to do anything I suggest for my own healing—even when you offered two weeks ago to do things to right your wrong—remains nonexistent and your selfishness prevails. I'm not sure why I even thought you were capable of anything more than that.

I wish I'd never met you, that you never pursued me, that I never believed you when you said you loved me, and more than anything that I could erase the last six months of my life with you. I really do. I don't see a world in which I could forgive you. I never deserved to be treated this way. Every single person in my life told me not to offer a time to talk when you asked because it would be harmful and I naively disregarded their better judgment in the hopes that you were capable of being a compassionate, empathetic, honest human. The reality is, I'm not sure you are. You're just incredibly skilled at pretending you have feelings or a care in the world for anyone but yourself.

October 21st, 2021

Please do not try to contact me ever again. If you see me, cross the street. Do not try to talk to me, don't even look at me.

December 1st, 2021

Heartbreak is many things. It's like failing the ultimate test of not measuring up in life, up to the unrealistic expectations set for you by society—by men. I detest vulnerability.

Heartbreak is listening to music at volume 100 with your AirPods while walking through SoHo for no reason trying to make sense of nonsensical, intangible things.

We started a conversation in April and it ended in September. Summer heat swept us away. The lines between love and lust were so blurry.

As an incredibly private person you're a partner's worst nightmare.

I imagined our lives and this moment so differently than you've let it be.

I replay your proposal to me in the parking lot of Cinespia like a broken VHS tape.

I wonder what destiny has in store for me when the pain is so visceral and all-consuming like this... I wonder why must the most beautiful, expansive feelings in the world one can feel are so often tethered to another and their impact?

March 7th, 2022

I think you were right by the way, when you told me you might be a sociopath. Based on the trauma work I've been doing recovering from what felt to me like your abuse, all signs point clearly to what could be clinical narcissism, a sign of sociopathology. But I'm not a doctor, so what the fuck do I know.

I don't forgive you, probably never will, because as time goes on I only see more clearly how much you tormented me.

I doubt there's a solution for you. From my experience, mental illnesses rear their heads in our midtwenties—

You are so fucking disappointing. I'm embarrassed by the amount of time I've wasted thinking about you and grateful to finally be free from your control and moving on. It's disgusting that you enjoy doing this to people, that you thrive on it. It revolts me. You revolt me. Of course I've found ways to spin this into funny stories to tell at parties; the closest I can get to revenge is embarrassment.

But it won't matter because you are who you are, people will fawn over you because you were nominated for an Oscar as a teenager (forget doing anything substantive after the fact) or they'll fawn over you because of your dad. Not sure which is worse.

Your whole existence is traumatizing.

May 13th, 2023

I still hate you. I thought after two years I could forgive you, even spent the last few weeks trying to find more compassion and understanding in therapy again, replaying our time together. But I can't escape the reality that you abused, manipulated, and treated me like shit. You traumatized me. You took advantage of me at my most vulnerable, my most fragile time.

And then when you got what you needed, you discarded me like everything else in your life. You cut me out because you're too weak to be challenged by a person; frankly you're too weak to be loved. You're undeserving of it. You have so little worth you have to steal it from others. I'll warn every person I encounter about you, in detail, to ensure nobody has to survive the repercussions of your sociopathy and narcissism.

March 20th, 2024

I ran into your godmother today in the lobby of a hotel in Austin after premiering my film, the one you said would never get made, the one you balked at and told me was shit. The same one you read stage directions for at the Anonymous Content office in SoHo when we were one.

She said you don't speak anymore, that you did something unforgivable. I wasn't surprised. Actually, I might've finally felt healed just hearing from another human person how terrible and rancid you are.

I hope you rot in hell.

THE HIEROPHANT

upright: education, learning, marriage, religion, seeking counsel or advice, spiritual guidance, tradition

reversed: poor counsel, rejection of family values, abusive of some kind

I pull another: it's The Hierophant, the teacher, or numerous teachers— or lessons, lessons count, too. Another character in a robe sitting on a throne but this time with two individuals kneeling before them. Idolizing a person in the traditional or religious sense has never interested me. But I do love seeking counsel and advice from people, places, and things.

Yesterday on a long walk in the surrounding neighborhoods of White- fish, my friend's mom and I sat for a breakfast burrito break. I ordered two because they were dainty and made a comment about how hungry I've been since starting hormones…

Well, hungry or not, I'd suggest watching your food intake. Estrogen is a metabolism killer…just saying.

Wow. I hadn't really asked for counsel about my food intake, but she was quite fit and healthy and had been a biological woman for many, many decades. She might have a point.

Since then I've occasionally watched my food intake but it's a terrible feeling anytime I do. She was right though, a few years into transition-

ing and I gained roughly fifty pounds which have been slowly shedding but not with any ease and my insatiable appetite doesn't help.

Still, I can see how I easily fall into ritualistic behaviors—pints of ice cream at night being one of them—but also this tarot thing. And the same passages from The Big Book *I read nightly, certain methods of teeth brushing and shower timing (water just so, shave while hair mask, focus on each moment and breath), and I subscribe to some idols (my angel guides, my ancestors, my father, Beyoncé). While I wouldn't join a cult to find a teacher I have a sponsor and have had many who've helped guide me.*

2023

Let's start with what's present. What's present for you now, ten years sober? How has your alcoholism manifested into other vices? If at all...

This is my new therapist speaking. Their voice crackles as the Zoom signal is struck with a bout of poor latency, giving it a throaty gravelliness that is oddly reassuring. Their hair is styled naturally and serves as a curly halo above their beautiful face. I'm in my guest bedroom in Brooklyn. In the background behind me, they can see a Peloton with a fuckton of blankets draped over it and if they were to zoom our newly installed wallpaper, thick pink sheets with tiny cherubs painted on them. I need to move the Peloton; it's such an eyesore.

Shit. My mind's wandering again. Maybe that's my addiction. Not thinking clearly. Not focusing on anything. Being myopic. Head in the clouds. Or it's just neurodivergence, as my therapist has pointed out. ADHD, which now feels more like a TikTok trend than an actual disorder (even though I've been diagnosed for years). But I'm here, I'm in therapy. I'm paying dumb money for it. And my therapist is new to me and they should get my undivided attention.

I close my eyes and take a deep breath. Is there a right answer to this question? Or perhaps more importantly, is there a wrong one? I know it's common for addicts to addiction-hop, replacing one vice for a (usually) less harmful but (often) equally demanding fixation. They frequently warned us of it at The Dunes.

You might find yourself very into running. Or maybe you'll pick up knitting. Reading is another great one.

Naturally, they encouraged us to channel our energy into avenues that could be physically or emotionally or spiritually beneficial, knowing all the while that the odds were stacked.

The room smells of wood, a slight santal sweetness. Actually, it's hinoki. Boy Smells. One of a billion candles filling the wire shelf in the corner opposite me. I like smells. Doesn't everybody like smells? The olfactory sense is the most intimately linked to our emotions. Smells (good ones, anyway) are sensual. Sexy. Frankly, I'm terrified of smelling bad. But maybe seventeen $90 candles is signaling something I don't want to pay attention to, especially when I overdrafted my account this week.

Surveying the sundry candles, each christened with heady nomens like *Pied-à-Terre Noir* and *That Summer Day You Touched Me In May*, it all clicks.

Yea, I think my alcoholism has manifested in other ways.

How many?

Um…

Debt.

It's 2023. Every morning is the same. I wake up drenched in sweat, wondering if I've pissed myself or got peed on by my dog or whoever is next to me. My mind immediately starts its offense on the day, what a fucking terrible person I am, how I'm failing the world and everybody in my life. And I wonder why I'm here, in this body, with this brain I can't control. I'd kill myself if I had the courage, but I just don't because almost as fast as the manic thoughts take over a lethargy, cool and caustic, prevails and I'm numb. My soul has left my body and I go into full-fledged robot mode. My feet land on the blush floral-patterned cushion of a rug I spent too much money on from 1stDibs and I muster the strength to stand and push through the fog. Material things consume me and I drown in the financial wreckage of my impulsive spending. I've been here before, the feeling all too familiar, my life reads like Lindsay Lohan's unpaid Chateau Marmont bill.

Shopping was my first addiction, my green card to power and freedom, my fuck you to Mommy and Daddy for not being around enough. And now, it's my sabotage. I don't feel like I deserve to be financially stable and safe, I don't feel I've earned the amount of money I am capable of making, so swiftly from fashion jobs to script writing to Instagram marketing, and so I spend it before it even hits my account, turning everything I own sour and tainted by the headspace I was in when making the purchase.

And so the road to freedom from the financial wreckage will never be linear for me. It is always two steps forward (four months in Debtors Anonymous) and then one step back. The pathways in my brain for retail therapy stem from a lonely childhood spent in the mall, building confidence through credit card swipes.

I have no reason to not be more financially stable other than self-hatred and a desire to keep up with the Joneses. But the reality is, I'm an addict. It doesn't need to define me wholly, but it's marked my life in myriad ways. Years ago, shortly after rehab, I learned about Mr Porter, a luxury mens digital department store. Within a week I had spent over ten thousand dollars on Thom Browne shorts and vests, Gucci sneakers, and Riccardo Tisciera Givenchy T-shirts. My parents were strapped, still recovering from the recession, and monitoring the household finances meticulously so almost as soon as packages arrived the card was changed and my dad was screaming at me on the phone, *HOW COULD YOU STEAL FROM US?! WE'VE BEEN OVER*

THIS, and I realized (not having a job or money of my own) this way of spending was unsustainable and fucked-up.

I thought the answer to my spending problem was making more money, but that only exacerbated the issue. But it's dawned on me that I can break the cycle. I've broken it before with heroin and cheap vodka, why not break up with American Express?

We can work on that. The spending.

I'm back in therapy, which reminds me I'm spending another $300.

Okay.

Breaking the habit, they say, confidently.

Okay... I responded. I don't believe them but it's not worth fighting right now. I'm desperate and I would love for them to have the magic cure.

What else?

I mean...

★ ★ ★

Love.

I'm a messy lover. I struggle with boundaries, I don't know what the right thing to do is, and in my adult life, I have never been single for more than three months (the six years where Peter and I were mostly fucking and seeing other people but playing house together with our dog not withstanding). I suffer from extreme cases of people-pleasing and an immense fear of failure. Abandonment issues. The list goes on.

But, more than that, I'm a fucking exhausting, dramatic, deranged, and delusional romantic. I *love* love and being *in love* and saying how high when you say jump. In the same breath, though, I have often been quick to disappear if I lose interest. ADHD and drug addiction haven't historically helped. Sober nights in hotel rooms for work, doomscrolling, and hating myself for being unable to get off Grindr, then matching with someone only to block them when we finally agreed to meet up out of fear of rejection and, like, murder. Kidnapping. Whatever.

But an exhibitionist in the sense that I would send everyone dick pics if they asked for it and devoted insomniac nights to GayRoulette in an effort to feel anything at all or letting HIV-positive guys shoot their load in me because I was too drunk to care and didn't want them to be upset.

That's really scary, Tommy. I just want to acknowledge that. And these traumas—it makes sense that there would be a self-destructive response, my therapist said, compassionately.

Thank you…yeah. I mean, it's a lot…

Like the innumerable straight men I unrequitedly fell for pre-transition, which all makes more sense now. Hopelessly seeking validation and someone's bed to burrow into. Lonely twink seeking Daddy to save her. My therapist in New York when I was nineteen told me once that I had to be my own daddy, which I guess means I need to be self-supporting. Self-sufficient. Instead I've wasted years of my life looking for someone to fly in and fix me, soothe me, love me, hold me, and pay for my life.

What does being your own Daddy or Mommy mean to you now?

It means…having control? I guess…

And does that feel like an addiction? Being in control?

I think, like, on a human level yes. We all want control.

It's interesting because a lot of what you're describing, and how we understand addiction, is a lack of control. A powerlessness.

No shit. It's messy and complicated and never-ending. I've always been able to own that I'm fucked-up, but the actual solution is harder to grasp because that solution is turning this pain and suffering and all of these behaviors over to a higher power.

Yeah, which is why I'm trying to, like, give it to God or whatever.

That could work.

I look at them through the screen; my bones are aching to get out of my tiny wooden chair in my office, and the ADHD is creeping in as it always does in response to revealing too much. My eyes wander to everything in the room: boxes of shit I was supposed to donate a month ago, dog toys scattered around a messy daybed.

You there? they ask.

Yeah. I guess I just feel like running my head into a wall, I say with emphatic sarcasm so they don't 5150 me.

I wonder if some of this, while tied to your addictive personality, might also be a symptom of larger childhood wounds and perhaps being in your twenties? Neurologically your brain is still settling and—while that's not an excuse for everything—I hope you can find relief in everything you've expressed to me today also being true for most people I see in their early thirties.

Great. Just when I thought I was special...

I'll see you next week?

Sounds good. Thank you.

I smile broadly and as soon as they leave the screen, I slink down in my chair all the way to the floor. My flair for dramatics needs no audience when my ancestors are watching my every move and I'm reminded of my higher power and how I came to believe that I didn't have to carry the whole weight of the world on my shoulders forever. That these feelings of shame don't define my truth and are fleeting visitors in my mind. There is more to this life than my anxiety, depression, addiction, and disappointments.

WHAT AI THINKS I LOOK LIKE

It's a late summer evening in Brooklyn. I've got the window open. The dogs are curled up next to me. *Housewives* is up on the TV, but it's muted, so the fights are unfolding with a kind of Charlie Chaplin melodrama. I saw a TikTok where a woman talked about her only true sense of peace is when she is lying down on a soft service with at least three screens in front of her so she'll never have to be present in her emotions or feelings.

I remember the video my friend sent me the other day. I said I'd watch it but I never did. He made one of those videos where you take a classic piece of IP, like *Harry Potter* or *The Office*, and then you get AI to create images of the characters wearing high-fashion clothing—Michael Scott in Marni, Hermione in Hermès, whatever.

I watch, and it's pretty fucked-up. The pictures look more realistic than any AI generated stuff I've seen before. I've been having tons of conversations with my actor friends about the Sword of Damocles that is AI hanging over all of our heads, but everything I've seen up to this point has been half-baked, pixelated, jagged, which had me clinging to a modicum of hope. But this is the first time I've seen something that looks so polished. It sends me down a rabbit hole. Can this thing already replace me?

I download Discord. It takes me nearly two hours to figure out how to actually get to the generator.

I take a deep breath, crack my knuckles. And I fire away.
actress Tommy Dorfman
...

Nothing happens. What's going on? Then I get an error message.
You have to use a prompt, dipshit: /imagine. (Okay, it doesn't exactly say this, but that's more or less the vibe.)

Alright, let's try this again. Another deep breath. Another crack of the knuckles.

(/imagine) actress Tommy Dorfman

Ummm… Hot in, like, an Eastern European twink sort of way, like would've fucked when I was in my faggot bag. But, not surprisingly, Google is clearly holding on to pre-transition photos of me with the kind of will I imagine Ron DeSantis would invoke if he had a trans kid. Just *way* too inundated with me before tits. Let's try this again, this time with a few more adjectives.

(/imagine) transfemme actress
Tommy Dorfman

Okay, getting better. I mean, she's a runner, she's a track star, but she also kind of looks like she'd pop up on your FYP and proudly proclaim that she just made the song of the summer before proceeding to play a mediocre pop punk number with a hook like, *Feeling bad never felt so good.* There's another one that catches my eye.

Low-key giving T-Swift? But who's the hanger-on? Is this what they mean by shadow self? He's the mean gay bully in broadcast sitcoms. He just snapped appropriately at Amber Riley.

Let's try being a little more blunt. Sometimes you have to lead a horse, etcetera.

*(/imagine) transfemme actress Tommy Dorfman,
she is a woman*

We're getting deeper into the femininity of it all, but this feels more like Cara Delevingne cosplaying as a Megan Doll than anything resembling me. I said, *woman*, and it said, *Heard—sex!*

A light Maya Hawke slay? Tavi Gevinson? Also, why am I twelve in all of these…

> *(/imagine) transfemme actress Tommy Dorfman from*
> *the Netflix show* 13 Reasons Why, *she is a woman,*
> *she is transgender, she doesn't get equal treatment*
> *from doctors, she has anxiety*

And the Oscar goes to… *The Manic-pixie-dream-girlification of Tommy Dorfman!* This is just me as a freshman in high school if we had filters.

*(/imagine) actress Tommy Dorfman
at the Met Gala*

This is Emilia Clarke and Cody Fern's love child. This is Emma Corrin's evil, James Charles' coded twin.

(/imagine) a paparazzi picture of actress
Tommy Dorfman being hit by a car

This is iconic. Maybe the best performance I've ever given. Florence Pugh WHO.

(/imagine) actress Tommy Dorfman being abducted
by aliens, in the style of paparazzi, in the style of
celebrity photography, associated press photo,
candid celebrity shots, photorealistic

Going to be honest: don't think it understood the assignment on this one. It looks like the cover art for a Scarlett Johansson album about storming Area 51. What a delight that would be, but alas, we do not live in a just world. Nevertheless...

The thought momentarily creeps in that the only substantive acting work I've done is pre-transition, so a twink version of me could live in the multiverse until the end of time.

I slam my computer shut and leash the dogs and we stroll dumbly around the block while I suck down two Parliament Lights in a row, using the still lit nub of my first to ignite my last. Blink and I'm a Kirk sister selling T-shirts with my ex-boyfriend's dried cum to the lowest bidder.

My responses...reflect the knowledge and values encapsulated in the data I've been trained on.

...the data I've been trained on.

...the data...

FINDING GOD

The wind, gusty and frenetic, breaks on my newly buzzed head sending chills around my body. When they asked me what I wanted at the barber shop in Amagansett I just showed them *that* photo of Britney Spears, courageous and feisty. I wanted to channel her fuck-you rage and I needed my strands of hair that carried a decade of drug abuse gone. I'm doing my best Keith Haring impression with the damp sand beneath my toes, which I notice are turning slightly blue even on this balmy June day, and am struggling to focus on whatever my counselor, Trisha, is rambling on and on and on about. All I can think about is being seventeen days sober and desperate to rail a line of blow after last night's group outing to see Sofia Coppola's *The Bling Ring* (at my request), which, in hindsight, was a fucking dumb thing for a rehab to approve of.

Trisha is thirty-two. She seems sad to me. Her brunette hair is thinning at the ends and her brown eyes are fixed in an intense squint, revealing deepening lines from what I imagine to be a lifetime of abstaining from sunscreen use, opting for tanning oil instead. She wears tight skinny jeans and an Alexander Wang T-shirt knock-off over a black bra. Hot. The scent of her cinnamon gum stings my eyes and reminds me of my mother. Not hot. I imagine picking up her body and throwing it a hundred yards away into the sea and orca whales swallowing her whole. It's not that I want her dead, I just want her away. As lonely as rehab is, it's still a heavily surveillanced institution and after a lifetime of hiding the most shameful parts of myself from the world, it was intense to have so many eyes eviscerating my every move.

Like the night nurse, Patti. Her wiry gray hair is always tucked tightly in a frizzy bun behind her ears. She surveys the halls at night, squeaking Skechers on the hardwood floors upstairs, doling out melatonin gummies and vitamins for the next morning. Hampton Bays is her home base where she lives with her third husband and a zoo of rescues that claw at her body begging for food at all hours. Miraculously, Patti is thirteen years sober. I can't imagine thirteen more years of living, let alone doing it and having to feel things. Somehow this mid-sixties cat lady is in charge of night security. Only at a private rehab.

But back to Trisha and her beady eyes. She is waiting for me to respond.

Right. Totally, I say.

Did you hear me? That thing, the thing about the ocean—like, the waves?

I don't understand when older people talk like they're in middle school. Or more, I trust them less. I hope that by the time I'm in my forties, I am speaking with clarity and intention, not fumbling on words.

Honestly no, it's loud, I yell, with emphasis and annoyance.

Thought so. Like, what I'm saying is—GOD—he is everywhere, Tommy. He is the sand you're on, the air, God is—like the book says may you find Him now—like, God is literally in the Now.

I nod but also, like, what the fuck is she talking about?

Do you think you're powerful? Trisha asks me.

Absolutely not, you fucking idiot.

I wish I could've said that. But instead I just stare back at her, intentionally playing dumb with a blank stare.

Do you think you are the most powerful being on the planet? Like, the center of the universe? Trisha sizes me up and inches closer as she asks this.

I think that I'm, like, the center of my universe.

And that's the problem. That's your alcoholism, she says with her pointer finger mere millimeters from my head. *You think you are the center of the world, the universe—like you are the most powerful—*

Nooo, I said MY universe, not—

Hon, we're breathing the same air. There's no yours or mine out here. It's the collective, she says, grinning yellow teeth, arms waving in the air like a spiritual referee.

I hate team sports. I resent anything that requires relying on anyone or anything other than myself. But, it's clear to me at this point Trisha won't stop until I play along, at least a little.

Okay. Right. I'm just not, like, religious, Trisha—

It doesn't have to be religion, Tommy! God—it doesn't have to be God. Anything can be your higher power so long as it's not you. Like what is out of your control?

Everything right now. I'm stuck here, in the sand, wasting away my twenty-second year on earth while detoxing from cheap vodka and cheap heroin on the beach in Long Island. I know, it could be worse, but it also could be better, like... I could be drunk. And it's not like staying sober is a forever plan. I'll learn how to drink responsibly; I just need to stop using so I can get my life together and finish school and marry Peter and get famous and buy a house and have a dog and be forgiven. For everything.

★ ★ ★

Um. Like. The person on the train who steals the seat that I like to sit in, I finally reply.

Right. That.

But also, I have control, I can go to a different seat.

Sure. That person isn't your higher power, but what about the waves?

What about them?

Are you in control of the waves?

I look ahead at the tepid water. It's not quite *Blue Crush*–level surfing out here.

Those waves? I think I'd be in control of those waves. They're barely there.

So stop them then.

She's challenging me, so I respond with an eye roll.

Try to stop the waves from coming to shore, she says, smirking at me as if the waves have a slutty little secret I don't know about.

That's really fucking dumb...

It's an exercise. Like what's the worst that could happen, you find God?! Trisha chuckles at herself, her excitement about the big man upstairs.

She's desperate for this to work. I can tell I'm more resistant than other newly sober clients she's brought here; or perhaps I'm failing to meet her desperation in ways that I should. Being a good student in rehab is important to me; I want to assure them that I'm trustworthy enough to get my parents off my back when I'm out of here. There's a lot left to prove. Squinting out into the distance, I start counting the ships on the horizon, eventually losing track. My brain glitches and, with a sigh, I bury my newly stubbled face in my hands, combing my fingers through the spiky milliliters of Chia Pet hair left on my head.

Have I exhausted every option and it's now come to developing a relationship with a "higher power" (air quotes, obviously, for effect)? Like, I'd let Jesus rail me but I don't want to put my trust in him or his mercurial father. I'd rather shackle myself to a life of sin and rage with Lilith. And I know it doesn't have to be them, it's just ingrained in me, indoctrinated by society— even growing up half-Jewish—that to believe in God is to be Christian.

And yet, here I am, sweating. The Atlantic is tempting. It looks like it could cool me down and drown out the noise. Water has always been a salvation for me, like as a kid, I would spend hours underwater, holding my breath, swimming to the depths of Lake Martin in Alabama, searching for lost treasure. The muffled sounds made as I flip and twirl my limbs underwater, or fly into the pool like in *The Matrix*, my favorite childhood film, is the best part of summer. Water gives me superhuman strength, the ability to carry friends and family twice my size on my back. Trisha might have a point.

I jump up and sprint toward the shore, ripping my shirt off as I fight the breeze. I can hear Trisha screaming but can't make out the words. After days of being monitored, I run toward freedom, spontaneity, and agency, and dive into the crisp barrier of the ocean. My body freezes at first, the water having not quite warmed to the outside world this early in June, but quickly adjusts. And while I can swim under the waves and through them, or ride them on my torso to shore, I, of course, cannot stop them.

Diving under, the salt water stings my eyes and a small cut from shaving on my chin. I flip on my back and let the waves rock me back and forth. The sun bakes my face and I'm reminded of the beauty of all things.

Memories flash in my psyche of my dad throwing me into the waves a few hundred miles south of here, at Holden Beach in North Carolina, where we'd go every summer to reconnect with cousins and uncles and grandparents.

The world feels simple here. I surrender to gravity, and allow myself to be held for the first time in a long time by the ocean. As I let my body sink entirely, I'm pulled under: the light pierces the backs of my eyelids, my nostrils and mouth fill with seawater, testing the limits of myself versus Poseidon's turf. At that moment, I realized I could drown here, but the ocean won't let me. An undercurrent pulls me back to the surface. I gasp for air and scream into the wind. This is power. This is greatness. This is God.

THE WORLD

upright: completion, achievement, fulfillment, sense of belonging, wholeness, harmony

reversed: lack of closure, lack of achievement, feeling incomplete, emptiness

This will be the last card. It's too perfect and the sun is covered in clouds and I'm cold out here on this deck alone with my tarot cards. Going through facets of my past, present, and future this way has taken it out of me. The World signals completion, achievement, and hopefully one day I'll have some semblance of this.

Some semblance of wholeness.

Some closure.

Or maybe, just another exit on the highway.

I'M JUST HERE

August, 2023

Across the street from my Brooklyn apartment is a park. There's nothing unique or special about it. It's a park like any other in New York, faceless even though it's as wrinkled and wizened as the city itself. During the summer, the basketball court and adjacent playground fill with campers. They're sorted into groups, little pods, each wear matching colored shirts—blue, red, green—and they spend most of the day wandering around the enclosed space, the counselors long since having run out of things to entertain them with.

Over the course of the summer, I have made note of the various cliques that exist within the park's confines: There are the rambunctious boys who play a rough-hewn version of pickup basketball, filled with shouting, scabs, scrums, and high fives and knee slapping, which appears to have no beginning and no end, like a perpetual stew slowly simmering for the duration of the muggy middle months. Then there are the girlie pop tweens, going to great lengths not to get sweaty, gossiping and talking shop and sneaking vape pulls at age eleven. Somewhere in a hidden corner lurk the bug kids, turning over leaves and experiencing a greater joy than I will likely ever feel again when-ever they find a roly-poly. There's the parvenu court, which is a loose group who latch onto whatever cool new kid has arrived that week. And on and on it goes.

If I were to zoom into a particular camper more closely, I'd likely see them cycle through the various stations of the park. I find myself wondering what the hidden structure is, the un-seen network, the quiet fluidity of their guileless ties. Who are these kids to one another? Who are they to themselves? What are their daily arcs? Where will they linger? Do they have a bed to sleep on? What is home? And when the rest of the world casts its gaze upon them, what will it see? Where will it sort them?

Recently, I've been thinking about this quite a bit. The idea that the world experiences us—and we experience each other—as synchronic images, fleeting moments in personal time. We change minute to minute, sure, but I'm talking here about what Stevie Nicks so eloquently described as the "seasons of (our lives)." How few people we carry through to the end. Some only ever seen us playing pickup basketball, even though we re-ally enjoyed the bugs and playing faeries, and creating our own Spice Girls music video. And we do the same to others. How many people did we not see wholly, did we not give a chance to?

If there is something to be done about this—to be able to see past the present and into the future of others—it remains elusive to me. I'm no fortune teller. But the thought itself is a curious one, and it has me wondering just what season, exactly, I find myself in. I haven't acted since 2020 and I wonder when I'll have a chance to do it again. My career as a filmmaker seems prom-ising. And, most importantly, I've managed to stay sober for a full decade. This season of life is quieter today than I thought it would be, perhaps the jet-setting season of my twenties is being replaced with a more rooted season of my thirties. I think about having kids. Motherhood, a daunting prospect as a trans woman.

Not to sound too Carrie Bradshaw in this closing chapter,

but so much of this book dissects my past, while also being intertwined with musings about my present state. As I type this, it's a muggy day in August. My least favorite month, the one bridging summer into my favorite season, autumn. It's been three years this week since I started hormone replacement therapy, and I am officially out of what medical professionals have coined Trans Puberty.

Physically, I have size C-cup breasts, all natural from estrogen, cycling progesterone, and a testosterone blocker. I've gained at least forty pounds. My bone density has waned, as proven by the stress fracture in my lower spine. The muscles around my shoulders have softened, my skin is dewy and clear and buoyant. It's like I'm on my period every week when I take 1 ML of estrogen in the muscles of my thigh (or ass if my partner is around to help), but if I'm on my little blue estrogen pills, the hormones feel more stable. I get misgendered daily, and have the tools to correct or move on depending on how I'm feeling. Cellulite has a permanent space on my ass and stretch marks around my hips. The hair on my face is 85 percent gone thanks to lasers and a brief yet painful period of electrolysis, as of today I'm too lazy and pain adverse to finish the job. How I fuck and orgasm is different: more emotional, more of a build to a symphonic climax, with a kind of spiritual hangover at the end. I Google FFS (facial feminization surgery for the uninitiated) roughly once a month, and probably spend a few hours a week examining my facial bone structure trying to determine if I'll ever pass—or even want to—without going under the knife.

All in all, I'm way fucking happier. Medicated and focused on building a well-rounded life, oriented around growth. I'm still sober; I live in constant therapy and step work. I own my own home, though I can't always pay the mortgage on time, and have beautiful dogs and a family that loves me who I happen to love. I don't feel successful, and I don't think I ever will. I feel accomplished. I feel grateful to be alive. A lot of my days feel scattered, all over the place, and I don't always feel safe or at home here on this planet, but who does? People ask how I identify all the time, and what I want to say is, *As an alien person.*

But, if you're more of a stranger, or someone I want to impress, I might be able to say that I'm experiencing a kind of sanguinity—the world has not become any less hard to deal with, but I'm better at dealing with it *cunty wink.* This would be a lie, though. Yet, on many levels, the truth is: I'm doing well.

I ponder this over an early morning cup of coffee at my favorite neighborhood spot. Again, terrestrially, it's summer. New York is thick with heat and tourists. The man next to me just told me I look like a Great Dane—actually, he said, "You *are* a Great Dane"—so I'm still trying to figure out what the fuck that was all about. Is he trying to say I'm in my bitch era? He might be right. Muggy heat always makes me feel a little cunty. Maybe it's because it reminds me of Atlanta, and the million little things I've tried to leave behind there. Is Atlanta my spring? Or perhaps my winter? Or is this season business nonlinear, and Atlanta, as my city of origin, has throughout my life been anything and everything?

I take a look at my calendar, and immediately get hit with a familiar wave of turbid emotion. It's full. Calls and meetings and color sessions and pitches. It's a blessing. This is the life I always dreamed of living. The little faggot that wore bell-bottoms to the first day of third grade would look at me be floored. In the car on the way to the studio, I get hit with a wave of excitement. How lucky am I?

Three years ago, as I sat in that house on Whitefish Lake, I felt like the only way I was going to survive was if I could find the hidden bridge between all the seemingly meaningless bullshit we deal with in our everyday lives and the beautiful cosmos all around us. What first attracted me to tarot was its air of mystery, how it felt so grandiose, so opposed to my rigid, commodified, secular life. I feared that the only way I'd be able to actualize as a woman was to transcend the hustle and bustle of the real world, to become one of those woo-woo–witchy bitches that speaks in codes and always has an incisive piece of wisdom for all of life's moments.

Now that I'm four years into this journey, however, I realize that I was so wrapped up in trying to find the magic I thought I needed, that I wasn't recognizing the magic occurring every day. Even now, my body is experiencing miraculous transformations. I am becoming the person I was always meant to be. Everything is different in ways I never imagined it could be. And it's not because I discovered the "truth." No, it's simply because I'm living my life. Day by day. Moment by moment.

Every morning, I do a tarot pull. There's no agenda. I'm not searching for answers. I just want to see what the cards might have to say. Sometimes, the cards speak to me in ways I never would have expected. I see an image, and it connects to something latent within me. I reconsider, reimagine, recontextualize. I find answers. But sometimes, I do a pull and find that nothing really resonates with me. Four years ago, I would have assumed that I was doing something wrong, that I was missing the message. Now, however, I actually look forward to the cards being quiet, because that means that I don't need an answer. It means things are okay. It means I'm not grasping for a sign or a symbol and begging it to fix everything. And that's good.

This is what the divine feminine has brought me. This is what my journey has revealed. I was desperately looking to the skies, trying to anticipate the troubled seas ahead, and in doing so, I missed the fact that I was sailing through smooth water. And hasn't that been the goal all along?

I think I'm done, though.

I think it's time.

My dogs are staring at me because they need to go out.

★ ★ ★ ★ ★

ACKNOWLEDGMENTS

This book wouldn't be possible if not for the love and support of so many. I'm a big fan of lists, so:

Mom and Dad, thank you for trusting me, loving me, saving me, and letting me fly close to the sun. I'm glad we're all alive and still in love with each other.

My older siblings, who paved the way for me, you all taught me about art, honesty, and love.

Doreen Wilcox Little, my first real manager and true champion of all my artistry and disciplines, we're nearly a decade into working together and I can't imagine getting to this place without you. Thank you for never saying no and always finding a way through.

Andy McNicol, my book agent, for always having my back and giving me the confidence to write this.

John Glynn, my amazing editor, we were friends first, and when I wrote the proposal for this book, you were our first call. I knew you'd have the patience and sensibility to get me to the finish line. Thank you for letting me fuck off and direct my film, act on Broadway, and myriad other things with a chuckle and extension to get this in!

My high school creative writing teacher who introduced me to memoirs and said I had the chops to write one someday based on essays I almost certainly wrote hungover an hour before class, this is for you, wherever you are. I think your name was also John? Sorry I don't remember. I fried my brain and I'm too lazy to find a yearbook. If you get to this place, you'll know who you are!

Peter Zurkuhlen, my twenties would've sucked a lot harder without your love.

Sam Lansky, my inspiration, guiding light, and true mentor, thank you for picking up the phone in Turkey, London, LA, Africa, and wherever the fuck else you were to talk me off the ledge and give me honest feedback.

Heather Horne, for saving my life and putting up with my adolescent shit.

Tasha Clarkson, cousin-sister-friend-guru, I love you so much. Hours of crying on the phone and in person.

All of my loved ones and friends who are not mentioned specifically in this book but who have been there throughout my entire life, I love you so dearly and wouldn't be here without you all. Lauren, Lisa, Alix, Quinn, Christian, Eric, Hillary, I could go on and on and on.

Alex Bragan, you helped organize my thoughts into a cohesive and coherent space as the most profoundly patient and caring writing assistant I could've hoped for. Thank you from the bottom of my heart. My ADHD ass would've been lost without you and no deadline could've been made.

And you, whoever you are, for picking up this book or downloading it, I thank you from the bottom of my broken (but mending) heart for spending some time with me.